AMERICAN POETS PROJECT

AMERICAN POETS PROJECT

IS PUBLISHED WITH A GIFT IN MEMORY OF

James Merrill

AND SUPPORT FROM ITS FOUNDING PATRONS

Sidney J. Weinberg, Jr. Foundation

The Berkley Foundation

Richard B. Fisher and Jeanne Donovan Fisher

Stephen C. Foster, c. 1859–60.

Stephen Foster & Co.

— LYRICS OF AMERICA'S FIRST GREAT POPULAR SONGS —

EDITED BY
KEN EMERSON

AMERICAN POETS PROJECT

THE LIBRARY OF AMERICA

To Deane Root, a great musicologist, mentor, and friend.

The paper used in this publication meets the minimum requirements of the American National Standard for Information Sciences—Permanence of Paper for Printed Library Materials, ANSI Z39.48—1984.

Design by Chip Kidd and Mark Melnick.

Library of Congress Control Number: 2009973459
ISBN 978-1-59853-070-4
American Poets Project—30

First Printing

Stephen
Foster
& Co.

Two minstrel archetypes: "Jim Crow" (c. 1832), by Thomas Dartmouth "Daddy" Rice, and "Zip Coon" (c. 1834), attributed to G. W. Dixon.

CONTENTS

PARLOR BALLADS

LIST OF ILLUSTRATIONS

INTRODUCTION

In 2009, as this anthology was being compiled, Bruce Springsteen and the E Street Band kicked off encores on their concert tour with a spirited rendition of "Hard Times Come Again No More," while in a Berkeley, California, supermarket I overheard a young mother console her fretful toddler by crooning, "Doo-dah! Doo-dah!" Not bad for a songwriter dead 145 years!

No other 19th-century American songwriter wrote even half as many songs remembered to this day as Stephen Collins Foster. They are so deeply imbedded in our culture that we take them and their composer for granted, as if Foster had been an all but anonymous folk poet when in fact he was our first successful full-time professional popular songwriter. As such he composed the first chapter in the Great American Songbook to which Irving Berlin, George Gershwin, and Bob Dylan, among so many others, have subsequently contributed. They knew in whose footsteps they were following. Berlin's first big hit asked, "Do you want to hear 'The Swanee River' played in ragtime?," and Gershwin's first great success, with lyrics by Irving Caesar, proclaimed, "Swanee, how I love you, how I love you . . ." Dylan, who has recorded "Hard Times Come Again No More," once told an interviewer, "I go back to Stephen Foster."

Like Berlin, Cole Porter, and Dylan, Foster wrote the words as well as the music to most of his songs, and the many drafts preserved in his workbook document how he labored over his lyrics. The best of them hold up and stand out independently on the page, even without a melody to drive them home. The eloquence, in "My Old Kentucky Home, Good-Night!," of "The day goes by like a shadow o'er the heart, / With sorrow where all was delight" is hard to surpass; so is the humorous hyperbole of horses "runnin' a race wid a shootin' star" in "De Camptown Races."

This collection includes the lyrics to 32 of the nearly 200 songs that Foster composed, and augments them with the words to another 49 songs, written between 1815 and 1890, that either influenced Foster or were influenced, as almost all later American popular music was, by his genius. That genius lay in Foster's ability to gather up the loose threads of the musical traditions that immigrants— enterprising, indentured, and enslaved—brought to a developing nation, and in his ambition to weave these threads into a distinctly American fabric, a quilt more coherent than crazy. In the lyrics that follow, and in the absent music that provides a ghostly accompaniment, you can hear the sprightly leaps of Scottish and Irish ballads, the urbanity of British music halls, the call-and-response of African and African-American song, the fluent melodies of Italian *bel canto*, the bounce of a Czech polka, even the sophistication of German *lieder*. (The introduction to one Foster song coyly quotes a Schubert serenade.) Multicultural more than a century before the term was coined, Foster was innovative, integrative, and all-American.

—

Born on July 4, 1826, America's first jubilee and the day John Adams and Thomas Jefferson died, Foster was a child of Jacksonian democracy, of an era in which politics, steamboats, railroads, the telegraph, lithography, high-speed rotary presses, and other improvements converged to make popular culture in general, and pop music in particular, possible. The passing of the old-guard elite, the education, enfranchisement and rise of the common man, and swifter, cheaper transportation and communication promoted vulgar, vigorous arts that appealed to many Americans—Whitman's "barbaric yawp"—rather than to a refined few. Steamboats bore popular songs and their performers—touring professional musicians or an amateur on other business able to captivate a tavern—from town to river town. Railroads subsequently opened up more venues. The telegraph whetted audiences' appetites by flashing to local newspapers advance word of the professional performers' rapturous reception at previous stops on their tours. (P. T. Barnum was an early if not the original master of the "humbug" we now call "publicity.") Folks who left the show humming a catchy new tune or were simply intrigued by its mention in the press could find the sheet music, frequently sporting an eye-catching illustrated cover emblazoned with a celebrity performer's name, in a music store, or the lyrics reprinted in cheap compilations known as "songsters." It wasn't the Internet, but word traveled faster and more widely than ever before, and pop music flourished.

Foster's father, a merchant, land speculator, and politician, had founded Lawrenceville, the suburb of Pittsburgh where Stephen was born, but soon lost his money and his home. Stephen, the Fosters' seventh offspring and the last to survive infancy, spent his childhood shunted from rentals to boarding houses to relatives around Pittsburgh and Ohio. Dropping out of college after only a week, Stephen showed little promise of reversing his family's downward spiral.

The slacker did have a knack for music, however. By age nine, he and other neighborhood boys were staging amateur theatricals in a carriage house and performing the rude, rowdy blackface songs that became the rage—and the first distinctly American popular music—in the late 1830s. Imagine that carriage house as the antebellum equivalent of a garage and think rock 'n' roll: Foster and his friends, like white American teenagers ever since, considered it cool to pretend they were black.

Foster's first known composition, written when he was 14, was a wordless waltz scored for three or four flutes. Soon he was writing his own minstrel songs and singing them with chums. One of these songs, "Away Down Souf," was entered in a contest at Pittsburgh's Eagle Ice Cream Saloon for the best "original words of an Ethiopian Melody." Although it failed to win the grand prize of a silver cup, the ice cream parlor's resident troupe was soon singing other Foster songs, including, on September 11, 1847, "Susanna." Within a year, "Oh! Susanna," as it became popularly known, was renowned from the mining camps of California to the concert halls of New York City. Foster quit his day job in Cincinnati, where he had been working as a bookkeeper for one of his brothers, returned to Pittsburgh, married Jane Denny McDowell, daughter of a local physician, and set up shop as a songwriter.

It was almost as audacious as if he had resolved to become an astronaut: the profession did not yet exist. Previous songwriters had supported themselves by performing, publishing, running a music store, giving music lessons, or all of the above. U.S. copyright law was rudimentary and often ignored. Between 1848 and 1850, at least 16 different publishers issued 30 different arrangements of "Oh! Susanna," and Foster may not have earned a single penny from them.

Foster contracted with publishers in Baltimore and New York. Sheet music generally sold for a quarter, and the New York firm of Firth, Pond & Co. promised two cents to Foster, who augmented this royalty by giving minstrel bandleader E. P. Christy first crack at performing his songs (and credit for composing "Old Folks at Home"). From the outset Foster wrote genteel parlor ballads as well as blackface minstrel songs. Only 10 percent of his life's work was written to be performed "*alla niggerando*," as the sheet music for one song noted with the brazen racism all too typical of the time. But Foster's "plantation melodies" vastly outsold delicate ballads such as "Ah! May the Red Rose Live Alway!," which fetched him just $8.12 in seven years. The success of "Beautiful Dreamer" was entirely posthumous.

". . . I had the intention of omitting my name on my Ethiopian songs," Foster wrote Christy, "owing to the prejudice against them by some, which might injure my reputation as a writer of another style of music, but I find that by my efforts I have done a great deal to build up a taste for the Ethiopian songs among refined people by making the words suitable to their taste, instead of the trashy and really offensive words which belong to some songs of that order."

Although some of Foster's blackface lyrics are abhorrent—the second verse of "Oh! Susanna" is a shocker—at their best they imbue African Americans with a dignity and pathos that were unprecedented. No songwriter had called a black woman a lady before "Nelly Was a Lady." Unbeknown to most of the throng that sings bowdlerized lyrics on Derby Day, "My Old Kentucky Home" does not celebrate cavaliers and crinolines in the Old South—it invokes *Uncle Tom's Cabin* and indicts slavery for breaking up black families.

Except during his stint in Cincinnati, Foster had little exposure to African Americans—Pittsburgh's black population amounted to only 714 in 1840—and even less to the South. Not until 1852 did he venture, for the first and only time in his life, farther south than Kentucky, traveling by steamboat to New Orleans and back. He never set eyes on the Suwannee River. But Foster's own experiences of homelessness and powerlessness enabled him to identify with African Americans and to project onto them his own anxieties. Even Frederick Douglass praised "My Old Kentucky Home" and "Uncle Ned" because they "can call forth a tear as well as a smile. They awaken sympathies for the slave, in which anti-slavery principles take root and flourish."

For a while Foster was as successful as a songwriter could conceivably have been, given the primitive state of the music business. From 1850 to 1857 his annual income averaged a little over $1,400—not bad when you consider that Andrew Carnegie's salary was raised to $1,500 when the Pennsylvania Railroad made him a division superintendent in 1859, but abysmal compared to the $1,000 a night that P. T. Barnum guaranteed Jenny Lind for the Swedish soprano's first American concert tour. And the erratic, unpredictable cash flow made it difficult to support a family comfortably or respectably. (Just shy of nine months after their wedding, the Fosters had a daughter, Marion.) The deaths of Foster's parents and a growing fondness for drink that Foster inherited from his father put additional strains on the marriage. Stephen and Jane separated and reunited several times. During one such separation Foster probably wrote "Jeanie with the Light Brown Hair," adapting his wife's nickname, Jenny.

By the 1860s, Foster was living alone in New York City in ever more abject circumstances. Although he had moved there to be closer to the center of the consolidating music industry, proximity did not restore his declining creative powers. Moreover, with one sister married to the younger brother of Doughface Democratic President James Buchanan and two other siblings harboring Copperhead animosity to Lincoln's Republican administration, Foster found it difficult to answer or echo the Civil War's call to arms. He wrote more prolifically, but less successfully, than ever before. Words came harder than melodies, so George Cooper (1840–1927), a young notary, minor poet, and would-be songwriter who befriended Foster, wrote the lyrics for more than 20 songs. Foster called him "the left wing of the song factory." One Sunday morning Cooper rushed to Foster's room in a Bowery hotel and found him naked, with a gash in his throat, a bruise on his forehead, and a burn on his thigh. Foster begged for a drink and died four days later on January 13, 1864. At 37 he was already a has-been. One of his few obituaries noted that his name "was once a household word throughout our land" but concluded that "he can hardly be said to have been more than an amateur writer."

The lyrics by songwriters other than Foster that flesh out this anthology are not an encyclopedic survey of 19th-century American song. They're a sampling of secular songs crafted for commercial purposes—in other words, pop music. They were chosen because the lyrics work independently on the page, while some of the most famous popular songs from the 19th century—George F. Root's "The

Battle Cry of Freedom," for instance, or Septimus Winner's "Listen to the Mocking Bird"—disappoint when denuded of their tunes. I have also tended to avoid poems that were subsequently set to music—Emma Willard's "Rock'd in the Cradle of the Deep," for example, or Julia Ward Howe's "Battle Hymn of the Republic"—in favor of words conceived from the outset as lyrics to particular melodies. The emphasis on commercial, secular songwriting inevitably leaves out hymns, songs in the folk tradition(s), and most lyrics by African Americans, who were with few exceptions excluded from the marketplace. Many of these lyrics are familiar but some of them, I hope, will surprise. I have been especially generous in my selections from the repertoire of the Hutchinson Family Singers and the musicals of Edward Harrigan and his father-in-law, David Braham, because they have been largely forgotten yet retain to this day a liveliness that is of far more than historical interest.

This anthology concludes a decade before the century did because the Columbian World Exhibition in Chicago ushered in a new era of popular music in 1893. This world's fair, the setting of Erik Larson's bestselling *The Devil in the White City*, introduced ragtime to the world and helped popularize Charles K. Harris's "After the Ball," an aggressively marketed ballad that sold hundreds of thousands if not a million copies in sheet music and is widely recognized as the first modern-day hit song. It was time to turn the page and begin a second chapter in the Great American Songbook.

Ken Emerson

PLANTATION MELODIES

A warning to all readers: Many of the lyrics immediately following are rated "R" for racist. They are "trashy and really offensive," as Foster complained, yet Foster himself on occasion was one of the greatest offenders. Not only the vocabulary—"n"-word and all—but the very idea of blackface minstrelsy is repellent. Yet minstrelsy spawned America's first distinctively indigenous and internationally influential popular songs. To this day we can hum many of their tunes if not recall their original words (sometimes ignorance is bliss). We can no more appreciate American music without understanding minstrelsy than we can grasp American history without acknowledging slavery.

Minstrelsy had antecedents in Micah Hawkins' songs celebrating American victories in the War of 1812 and in the skits of visiting British comedian Charles Matthews, but it did not acquire an identity or impetus until the late 1820s, when George Washington Dixon (c. 1801–1861) and Thomas Dartmouth "Daddy" Rice (1808–1860) began performing sketches and songs that mocked an uppity black dandy (Dixon's Zip Coon) and a raggedy gimp (Rice's Jim Crow).

The solo acts of these "Ethiopian delineators" were succeeded by the full-blown minstrel band and evening-long show, which the Virginia Minstrels introduced in 1843. Led by Daniel Decatur Emmett (1815–1904) on fiddle, the three other Virginia Minstrels, all of them in burnt cork, woolly wigs, and tawdry rags, plied the banjo, tambourine, and bones. Although they broke up within a year, while touring England, their "horrible noise" provoked a worldwide sensation, a host of imitators (including Stephen Foster), and a roisterous musical tradition that persisted deep into the 20th century. Emmett, who wrote the words for the Virginia Minstrels' most popular number, "Old Dan Tucker," went on to compose "I Wish I Was in Dixie's Land" and many other minstrel songs.

Without for a moment denying the racism inherent in minstrelsy, it's important to note that the mask of blackface was a means not only of reinforcing racial, social, and economic norms but also, at times, of escaping or rebelling against them. Minstrel performers and audiences, mostly from the rapidly industrializing Northeast and Midwest, knew next to nothing about slavery down South. Yet they recognized parallels between the plantation fields and the factory floor; it was during 1830s and 1840s that the terms "white slavery" and the "slavery of wages" entered the national discourse. And many recent arrivals to America's burgeoning cities felt pangs of nostalgia for life on the farm they had left behind, in the States or the old country. For these complicated and often contradictory reasons, minstrel songs, in addition to deriding African Americans, sometimes sympathized and identified with them.

Thus Henry Clay Work (1832–1884), a versatile songwriter and fervent Unionist who achieved his greatest success during the Civil War, used blackface dialect to celebrate the liberation of slaves in "Kingdom Coming," composed for Christy's Minstrels. Nor is there anything demeaning (apart from the word "darkey") in the admiration the songwriter known only by the initials "J. K." expresses for a mulatto belle in "The Yellow Rose of Texas."

Minstrelsy remained popular after the Civil War. Even African Americans "blacked up." For several decades the form's outstanding composer was a black man, James

A. Bland (1854–1911), whose singing, dancing, and acrobatic stunts were highly acclaimed in England (where he performed with Haverly's Genuine Colored Minstrels) as well as in the United States. Bland's debt to Foster was profound. His most famous song, "Carry Me Back to Old Virginny," follows the nostalgic formula of "Old Folks at Home," while "In the Evening by the Moonlight" echoes "My Old Kentucky Home"—almost word for word in "so merry gay and bright."

At the end of the 19th century, as Jim Crow racial restrictions grew more oppressive throughout much of the nation, minstrel songs were in large measure supplanted by so-called "coon songs," which set to spikier ragtime rhythms nastier lyrics in which African Americans toted razors more frequently than they strummed banjos. Minstrelsy lingered on in many forms during the 20th century —in Al Jolson's stentorian mammy songs, in Johnny Mercer's lazybones lyrics, in the Hollywood musicals of Judy Garland, Mickey Rooney, and Fred Astaire, in the "Dream Songs" of poet John Berryman. Gradually, increasing racial awareness and sensitivity all but outlawed the most overt manifestations of blackface, but white performers and listeners have embraced rock 'n' roll, reggae, and rap in a recurring process in which racism, rip-off, emulation, and admiration become as blurred as the tiger stripes in *Little Black Sambo*. Indeed, such love and theft, in the words Bob Dylan plucked from historian Eric Lott, are still so deep a current in popular and American culture that they almost define them.

STEPHEN C. FOSTER

Lou'siana Belle

Oh! Lou'siana's de same old state,
Whar Massa us'd to dwell;
He had a lubly cullud gal.
'Twas the Lou'siana Belle.

<small>CHORUS</small>
Oh! Belle don't you tell, don't tell Massa, don't you Belle,
Oh! Belle, de Lou'siana Belle, I's gwine to marry you
      Lou'siana Belle.

2

I went to de ball de udder night,
I cut a mighty swell;
I danc'd de Polka pigeon wing,
Wid de Lou'siana Belle.

3

Dere's Dandy Jim ob Caroline
I knows him by de swell,
Tryin to come it mighty fine,
Wid de Lou'siana Belle.

4

Dere's first de B and den de E,
And den de double LL;
Anodder E to the end ob dat,
Spells Lou'siana Belle.

1847

Uncle Ned

Dere was an old Nigga, dey call'd him Uncle Ned
He's dead long ago, long ago!
He had no wool on de top ob his head
De place whar de wool ought to grow.

CHORUS
Den lay down de shubble and de hoe.
Hang up de fiddle and de bow:
No more hard work for poor Old Ned
He's gone whar de good Niggas go.
No more hard work for poor Old Ned
He's gone whar de good Niggas go.

2

His fingers where long like de cane in de brake,
He had no eyes for to see;
He had no teeth for to eat de corn cake
So he had to let de corn cake be.

3

When Old Ned die Massa take it mighty bad,
De tears run down like de rain;
Old Missus turn pale, and she gets berry sad
Cayse she nebber see Old Ned again.

1848

Susanna

I come from Alabama with my Banjo on my knee
I'se gwine to Lou'siana my true lub for to see.
It rain'd all night de day I left, de wedder it was dry;
The sun so hot I froze to def Susanna, don't you cry.

Oh! Susanna, do not cry for me;
I come from Alabama, wid my Banjo on my knee.

2

I jump'd aboard the telegraph and trabbled down de ribber,
De lectrick fluid magnified, and kill'd five hundred Nigga.
De bulgine bust and de hoss ran off, I really thought I'd
    die;
I shut my eyes to hold my bref Susanna don't you cry.

3

I had a dream de udder night, when ebry ting was still;
I thought I saw Susanna dear, a coming down de hill,
De buckwheat cake was in her mouf, de tear was in her
    eye,
I says, I'se coming from de souf Susanna don't you cry.

1848

Away Down Souf

We'll put for de souf Ah! dat's the place,
For the steeple chase and de bully hoss race
Poker, brag, eucher, seven up and loo,
Den chime in Niggas, wont you come along too.

CHORUS
No use talkin when de Nigga wants to go,
Whar de corn-top blossom and de canebrake grow;
Den come along to Cuba, and we'll dance de polka juba,
Way down souf, whar de corn grow.

2

My lub she hab a very large mouf,
One corner in de norf, tudder corner in de souf;
It am so long, it reach so far
Trabble all around it on a railroad car.

3

I went last night to see my Sally
Two story house in Pigtail ally,
Whar de skeeters buz, and de fleas dey bite,
And de bull dogs howl and de tom cats fight.

1848

Nelly Was a Lady

Down on de Mississippi floating,
Long time I trabble on de way,
All night de cottonwood a toting,
Sing for my true-lub all de day.

Nelly was a lady
Last night she died,
Toll de bell for lubly Nell
My dark Virginny bride.

2

Now I'm unhappy and I'm weeping,
Can't tote de cotton-wood no more;
Last night, while Nelly was a sleeping,
Death came a knockin at de door.

3

When I saw my Nelly in de morning,
Smile till she open'd up her eyes,
Seem'd like de light ob day a dawning,
Jist 'fore de sun begin to rise.

4

Close by de margin ob de water,
Whar de lone weeping willow grows,
Dar lib'd Virginny's lubly daughter;
Dar she in death may find repose.

5

Down in de meadow mong de clober,
Walk wid my Nelly by my side;
Now all dem happy days am ober,
Farewell my dark Virginny bride.

1849

Nelly Bly

Nelly Bly! Nelly Bly! bring de broom along,
We'll sweep de kitchen clean, my dear, and hab a little
    song.
Poke de wood, my lady lub, and make de fire burn,
And while I take de banjo down, just gib de mush a turn.

CHORUS
Heigh! Nelly Ho! Nelly, listen lub to me,
I'll sing for you play for you, a dulcem melody.
Heigh! Nelly, Ho! Nelly, listen lub to me,
I'll sing for you, play for you a dulcem melody.

2
Nelly Bly hab a voice like de turtle dove,
I hears it in de meadow and I hears it in de grove.
Nelly Bly hab a heart warm as cup ob tea,
And bigger dan de sweet potato down in Tennessee.

3

Nelly Bly shuts her eye when she goes to sleep,
When she wakens up again her eyeballs gin to peep.
De way she walks, she lifts her foot, and den she brings
    it down,
And when it lights der's music dah in dat part ob de town.

4

Nelly Bly! Nelly Bly! nebber, nebber sigh,
Nebber bring de tear drop to de corner ob your eye,
For de pie is made ob punkins and de mush is made ob
    corn,
And der's corn and punkins plenty lub a lyin in de barn.

1850

"Gwine To Run All Night," or De Camptown Races

De Camptown ladies sing dis song
Doo-dah! doo-dah!
De Camptown race-track five miles long
Oh! doo-dah day!
I come down dah wid my hat caved in
Doo-dah! doo-dah!
I go back home wid a pocket full of tin
Oh! doo-dah day!

CHORUS

Gwine to run all night!
Gwine to run all day!
I'll bet my money on de bob-tail nag
Somebody bet on de bay.

2

De long tail filly and de big black hoss
Doo-dah! doo-dah!
Dey fly de track and dey both cut across
Oh! doo-dah-day!
De blind hoss sticken in a big mud hole
Doo-dah! doo-dah!
Can't touch bottom wid a ten foot pole
Oh! doo-dah-day!

3

Old muley cow come on to de track
Doo-dah! doo-dah!
De bob-tail fling her ober his back
Oh! doo-dah-day
Den fly along like a rail-road car
Doo-dah! doo-dah!
Runnin' a race wid a shootin' star
Oh! doo-dah-day!

4

See dem flyin' on a ten mile heat
Doo-dah! doo-dah!
Round de race track, den repeat
Oh! doo-dah-day!
I win my money on de bob-tail nag
Doo-dah! doo-dah!
I keep my money in an old tow-bag
Oh! doo-dah-day!

1850

Angelina Baker

Way down on de old plantation
  Dah's where I was born,
I used to beat de whole creation
  Hoein' in de corn:
Oh! den I work and den I sing
  So happy all de day,
Till Angelina Baker came
  And stole my heart away.

CHORUS
Angelina Baker! Angelina Baker's gone
She left me here to weep a tear
And beat on de old jawbone.

2

I've seen my Angelina
  In de spring-time and de fall,
I've seen her in de corn-field
  And I've seen her at de ball;
And ebry time I met her
  She was smiling like de sun,
But now I'm left to weep a tear
  Cayse Angelina's gone.

3

Angelina am so tall
  She nebber sees de ground,
She hab to take a wellumscope
  To look down on de town

Angelina likes de boys
   As far as she can see dem,
She used to run old Massa round
   To ax him for to free dem.

   4

Early in de morning
   Ob a lubly summer day
I ax for Angelina,
   And dey say "she's gone away"
I don't know wha to find her,
   Cayse I don't know wha she's gone,
She left me here to weep a tear
   And beat on de old jawbone.

1850

Ring, Ring de Banjo!

De time is nebber dreary
   If de darkey nebber groans;
De ladies nebber weary
   Wid de rattle ob de bones:
Den come again Susanna
   By de gaslight ob de moon;
We'll tum de old Piano
   When de banjo's out ob tune.

CHORUS
Ring, ring de banjo!
I like dat good old song,

Come again my true lub,
Oh! wha you been so long.

2

Oh! nebber count de bubbles
  While der's water in de spring:
De darkey hab no troubles
  While he's got dis song to sing.
De beauties ob creation
  Will nebber lose der charm
While I roam de old plantation
  Wid my true lub on my arm.

3

Once I was so lucky,
  My massa set me free,
I went to old Kentucky
  To see what I could see:
I could not go no farder,
  I turn to massa's door,
I lub him all de harder,
  I'll go away no more.

4

Early in de morning
  Ob a lubly summer day,
My massa send me warning
  He'd like to hear me play.
On de banjo tapping,
  I come wid dulcem strain;
Massa fall a napping—
  He'll nebber wake again.

My lub, I'll hab to leabe you
  While de ribber's running high:
But I nebber can desceibe you—
  So dont you wipe your eye.
I's guine to make some money;
  But I'll come anodder day—
I'll come again my honey,
  If I hab to work my way.

1851

Old Folks at Home

Way down upon de Swanee ribber,
Far, far away,
Dere's wha my heart is turning ebber,
Dere's wha de old folks stay.
All up and down de whole creation,
Sadly I roam,
Still longing for de old plantation,
And for de old folks at home.

CHORUS
All de world am sad and dreary,
Ebry where I roam,
Oh! darkeys how my heart grows weary,
Far from de old folks at home.

2

All round de little farm I wandered
When I was young,

Den many happy days I squandered,
Many de songs I sung.
When I was playing wid my brudder,
Happy was I—
Oh! take me to my kind old mudder,
Dere let me live and die.

3

One little hut among de bushes,
One dat I love,
Still sadly to my mem'ry rushes,
No matter where I rove.
When will I see de bees a humming,
All round de comb?
When will I hear de banjo tumming,
Down in my good old home?

1851

Massa's in de Cold Ground

Round de meadows am a ringing
De darkeys' mournful song,
While de mockingbird am singing,
Happy as de day am long.
Where de ivy am a creeping
O'er de grassy mound,
Dare old massa am a sleeping,
Sleeping in de cold, cold ground.

Down in de corn-field
Hear dat mournful sound:
All de darkeys am a weeping
Massa's in de cold, cold ground.

2

When de autumn leaves were falling,
When de days were cold,
'Twas hard to hear old massa calling,
Cayse he was so weak and old.
Now de orange tree am blooming
On de sandy shore,
Now de summer days am coming,
Massa nebber calls no more.

3

Massa made de darkeys love him,
Cayse he was so kind,
Now dey sadly weep above him,
Mourning cayse he leave dem behind.
I cannot work before tomorrow,
Cayse de tear drops flow,
I try to drive away my sorrow
Pickin on de old banjo.

1852

My Old Kentucky Home, Good-Night!

The sun shines bright in the old Kentucky home,
'Tis summer, the darkies are gay,
The corn top's ripe and the meadow's in the bloom
While the birds make music all the day.
The young folks roll on the little cabin floor,
All merry, all happy and bright:
By'n by Hard Times comes a knocking at the door,
Then my old Kentucky Home, good night!

CHORUS
Weep no more, my lady, oh! weep no more today!
We will sing one song
For the old Kentucky Home,
For the old Kentucky Home, far away.

2

They hunt no more for the possum and the coon
On the meadow, the hill and the shore,
They sing no more by the glimmer of the moon,
On the bench by the old cabin door.
The day goes by like a shadow o'er the heart,
With sorrow where all was delight:
The time has come when the darkies have to part,
Then my old Kentucky Home, good-night!

3

The head must bow and the back will have to bend,
Wherever the darkey may go:
A few more days, and the trouble all will end

In the field where the sugar-canes grow.
A few more days for to tote the weary load,
No matter 'twill never be light,
A few more days till we totter on the road,
Then my old Kentucky Home, good-night!

1853

The Glendy Burk

De Glendy Burk is a mighty fast boat,
Wid a mighty fast captain too;
He sits up dah on de hurricane roof
And he keeps his eye on de crew.
I cant stay here, for dey work too hard;
I'm bound to leave dis town;
I'll take my duds and tote 'em on my back
When de Glendy Burk comes down.

CHORUS
Ho! for Lou'siana!
I'm bound to leave dis town;
I'll take my duds and tote 'em on my back
When de Glendy Burk comes down.

2

De Glendy Burk has a funny old crew
And dey sing de boatman's song,
Dey burn de pitch and de pine knot too,
For to shove de boat along.
De smoke goes up and de ingine roars

And de wheel goes round and round,
So fair you well! for I'll take a little ride
When de Glendy Burk comes down.

3

I'll work all night in de wind and storm,
I'll work all day in de rain,
Till I find myself on de levy dock
In New Orleans again.
Dey make me mow in de hay field here
And knock my head wid de flail,
I'll go wha dey work wid de sugar and de cane
And roll on de cotton bale.

4

My lady love is as pretty as a pink,
I'll meet her on de way
I'll take her back to de sunny old south
And dah I'll make her stay
So don't you fret my honey dear,
Oh! don't you fret Miss Brown
I'll take you back 'fore de middle of de week
When de Glendy Burk comes down.

1860

Old Black Joe

Gone are the days when my heart was young and gay,
Gone are my friends from the cotton fields away,
Gone from the earth to a better land I know,
I hear their gentle voices calling "Old Black Joe."

I'm coming, I'm coming, for my head is bending low:
I hear those gentle voices calling, "Old Black Joe."

2

Why do I weep when my heart should feel no pain
Why do I sigh that my friends come not again,
Grieving for forms now departed long ago?
I hear their gentle voices calling "Old Black Joe."

3

Where are the hearts once so happy and so free?
The children so dear that I held upon my knee,
Gone to the shore where my soul has longed to go.
I hear their gentle voices calling "Old Black Joe."

1860

THOMAS DARTMOUTH "DADDY" RICE

Jim Crow

Come listen all you galls and boys,
    I's jist from Tuckyhoe,
I'm goin to sing a little song,
    My name's Jim Crow.

CHORUS
Weel about and turn about and do jis so,
Eb'ry time I weel about and jump Jim Crow.

Oh I'm a roarer on de Fiddle,
   And down in old Virginny,
They say I play de skyentific
   Like Massa Pagannini.

I git 'pon a flat boat,
   I cotch de Uncle Sam,
Den I went to see de place
   Where dey kill'd Packenham.

I went down to de riber,
   I didn't mean to stay,
But dere I see so many galls,
   I couldn't get away.

And den I go to Orleans
   An feel so full of fight
Dey put me in de Calaboose,
   An keep me dere all night.

When I got out I hit a man,
   His name I now forget,
But dere was nothing left
   'Sept a little grease spot.

7

I wip my weight in wildcats
　　I eat an Alligator,
And tear up more ground
　　Dan kiver 50 load of tater.

8

I sit upon a Hornet's nest,
　　I dance upon my head,
I tie a Wiper round my neck
　　And den I goes to bed.

9

Dere's Possum up de gumtree,
　　An Raccoon in de hollow,
Wake Snake for June bugs
　　Stole my half a dollar.

10

A ring tail'd monkey,
　　An a rib nose Babboon,
Went out de odder day
　　To spend de arternoon.

11

Oh de way dey bake de hoe cake
　　In old Virginny neber tire,
Dey put de doe upon de foot,
　　An hole it to de fire.

12

Oh by trade I am a carpenter,
    But be it understood,
De way I get my liben is,
    By sawing de tick oh wood.

13

I'm a full blooded niggar,
    Ob de real ole stock,
An wid my head and shoulder
    I can split a horse block.

14

I struck a Jarsey niggar,
    In de street de oder day,
An I hope I neber stir,
    If he didn't turn gray.

15

I'm berry much afraid of late,
    Dis jumping will be no good,
For while de Crow are dancing,
    De Wites will saw de wood.

16

But if dey get honest,
    By sawing wood like slaves,
Dere's an end to de business,
    Ob our friend Massa Hays.

17

I met a Philadelphia niggar,
    Dress'd up quite & clean,
But de way 'bused de Yorkers,
    I thought was berry mean.

18

So I knocked down dis Sambo,
    And shut up his light,
For I'm jist about as sassy,
    As if I was half white.

19

But he soon jumped up again,
    An 'gan for me to feel,
Says I go away you niggar,
    Or I'll skin you like an eel.

20

I'm so glad dat I'm a niggar,
    And don't you wish you was too,
For den you'd gain popularity,
    By jumping Jim Crow.

21

Now my brodder niggars,
    I do not think it right,
Dat you should laugh at dem,
    Who happen to be white.

22

Kase it dar misfortune,
    And dey'd spend ebery dollar,
If dey only could be
    Gentlemen ob colour.

23

It almost break my heart,
    To see dem envy me,
And from my soul I wish dem,
    Full as black as we.

24

What stuff it is in dem,
    To make de Debbil black
I'll prove dat he is white,
    In de twinkling of a crack.

25

For you see loved brodders,
    As true as he had a tail,
It is his berry wickedness,
    What makes him turn pale.

26

I went to Hoboken,
    To hab a promenade,
An dar I see de pretty gals,
    Drinking de Lemonade.

27

Dat sour and dat sweet,
　　Is berry good by gum,
But de best of lemonade is,
　　Made by adding rum.

28

At de Swan cottage,
　　Is de place I tink,
What dey make dis 'licious,
　　An 'toxicating drink.

29

Some go to Weehawk,
　　An some to Brooklyn hight,
But dey better stay at home,
　　If dey want to see de sight.

30

To go to de museum,
　　I'm sure it is dere duty,
If for noting else,
　　Jist to see de sleeping beauty.

31

An dere is daddy Lambert,
　　An a skeleton on he hunkie,
An likeness of Broadway dandy,
　　In a glass case of monkies.

32

De Broadway bells,
   When dey carry full sail,
Around dem wear a funny ting,
   Just like a fox tail.

33

When you hear de name of it,
   I sure it make you roar,
Why I ax'd 'em what it was,
   And dey said it was a boar.

34

De great Nullification,
   And fuss in de South,
Is now before Congress,
   To be tried by word ob mouth.

35

Dey hab had no blows yet,
   And I hope dey nebber will,
For its berry cruel in bredren,
   One anoders blood to spill.

36

Wid Jackson at de head,
   Dey soon de ting may settle
For ole Hickory is a man,
   Dat's tarnal full ob mettle.

37

Should dey get to fighting,
   Perhaps de blacks will rise,
For deir wish for freedom,
   Is shining in deir eyes.

38

An if de blacks should get free,
   I guess dey'll fee some bigger,
An I shall concider it,
   A bold stroke for de niggar.

39

I'm for freedom,
   An for Union altogether,
Aldough I'm a black man,
   De white is call'd my broder.

40

I'm for a union to a gal,
   An dis is a stubborn fact,
But if I marry an don't like it,
   I'll nullify de act.

41

I'm tired of being a single man,
   An I'm 'tarmined to get a wife,
For what I think de happiest,
   Is de swee married life.

42

Its berry common 'mong de white,
   To marry and get divorced,
But dat I'll nebber do,
   Unless I'm really forced.

43

I think I see myself in Broadway,
   Wid my wife upon my arm,
And to follow up de fashion,
   Dere sure can be no harm.

44

An I caution all white dandies,
   Not to come in my way,
For if dey insult me,
   Dey'll in de gutter lie.

c. 1832

GEORGE WASHINGTON DIXON

Zip Coon

O ole Zip Coon he is a larned skolar,
O ole Zip Coon he is a larned skolar,
O ole Zip Coon he is a larned skolar,
Sings posum up a gum tree an coony in a holler,
Posum up a gum tree, coony on a stump,
Posum up a gum tree, coony on a stump,

Posum up a gum tree coony on a stump,
Den over dubble trubble, Zip Coon will jump.

O Zip a duden duden duden zip a duden day.
O Zip a duden duden duden duden duden day.
O Zip a duden duden duden duden duden day.
Zip a duden duden duden zip a duden day.

2

O its old Suky blue skin, she is in lub wid me
I went the udder arter noon to take a dish ob tea;
What do you tink now, Suky hab for supper,
Why chicken foot an posum heel, widout any butter.

3

Did you eber see the wild goose, sailing on de ocean,
O de wild goose motion is a bery pretty notion;
Ebry time de wild goose, beckens to de swaller,
You hear him google google google google gollar.

4

I went down to Sandy Hollar t other arternoon
And the first man I chanced to meet war ole Zip Coon;
Ole Zip Coon he is a natty scholar,
For he plays upon de Banjo "Cooney in de hollar."

5

My old Missus she's mad wid me,
Kase I wouldn't go wid her into Tennessee
Massa build him barn and put in de fodder
Twas dis ting and dat ting one ting or odder.

6

I pose you heard ob de battle New Orleans,
Whar ole Gineral Jackson gib de British beans;
Dare de Yankee boys do de job so slick,
For dey cotch old Packenham an rowed him up de creek.

7

I hab many tings to tork about, but dont know wich
    come first,
So here de toast to old Zip Coon before he gin to rust;
May he hab de pretty girls, like de King ob ole,
To sing dis song so many times, 'fore he turn to mole.

c. 1834

My Long Tail Blue

I've come to town to see you all,
    I ask you how d'ye do?
I'll sing a song not very long,
    About my long tail blue.

CHORUS
Oh! for the long tail blue.
Oh! for the long tail blue.
I'll sing a song not very long
About my long tail blue.

2

Some Niggers they have but one coat,
    But you see I've got two;
I wears a jacket all the week,
    And Sunday my long tail blue.

3

Jim Crow is courting a white gall,
    And yaller folks call her Sue;
I guess she back'd a nigger out,
    And swung my long tail blue.

4

Jim Crow got mad and swore he'd fight,
    With sword and pistol too;
But I guess I back'd the nigger out,
    When he saw my long tail blue.

5

As I was gwoin up Market Street,
    I holler'd arter Sue,
The watchman came and took me up,
    And spilte my long tail blue.

6

I took it to a Tailor's shop,
    To see what he could do;
He took a needle and some thread,
    And mended my long tail blue.

7

If you want to win the Ladie's hearts,
    I'll tell you what to do;
Go to a tip top Tailor's shop,
    And buy a long tail blue.

Now all you chaps that wantsa wife,
   And don't know how to do;
Just look at me and I'll show you how,
   For to swing your long tail blue.

c. 1834

DANIEL DECATUR EMMETT

Old Dan Tucker

I come to town de udder night,
I hear de noise an saw de fight,
De watchman was a runnin roun,
Cryin Old Dan Tucker's come to town,

CHORUS
So get out de way! get out de way! get out de way!
Old Dan Tucker your to late to come to supper.

    2
Tucker is a nice old man,
He use to ride our darby ram;
He sent him whizzen down de hill,
If he hadn't got up he'd lay dar still.

3

Here's my razor in good order
Magnum bonum—jis hab bought 'er;
Sheep shell oats, Tucker shell de corn,
I'll shabe you soon as de water get warm.

4

Ole Dan Tucker an I got drunk,
He fell in de fire an kick up a chunk,
De charcoal got inside he shoe
Lor bless you honey how de ashes flew.

5

Down de road foremost de stump,
Massa make me work de pump;
I pump so hard I broke de sucker,
Dar was work for ole Dan Tucker.

6

I went to town to buy some goods
I lost myself in a piece of woods,
De night was dark I had to suffer,
It froze de heel of Daniel Tucker.

7

Tucker was a hardened sinner,
He nebber said his grace at dinner;
De ole sow squeel, de pigs did squall
He 'hole hog wid de tail and all.

1843

I Wish I Was in Dixie's Land

I wish I was in de land ob cotton,
Old times dar am not forgotten;
   Look away! Look away! Look away! Dixie Land.
In Dixie Land whar I was born in,
Early on one frosty mornin,
   Look away! Look away! Look away! Dixie Land.

CHORUS
Den I wish I was in Dixie, Hooray! Hooray!
In Dixie Land, I'll took my stand,
To lib an die in Dixie,
Away, Away, Away down south in Dixie,
Away, Away, Away down south in Dixie.

2

Old Missus marry "Will-de-weaber,"
Willium was a gay deceaber;
   Look away! &c.
But when he put his arm around 'er,
He smiled as fierce as a 'forty-pound'er.
   Look away! &c.

3

His face was sharp as a butchers cleaber,
But dat did not seem to greab' er;
   Look away! &c.
Old Missus acted de foolish part,
And died for a man dat broke her heart.
   Look away! &c.

4

Now here's a health to the next old Missus,
An all de galls dat want to kiss us;
    Look away! &c.
But if you want to drive 'way sorrow,
Come an hear dis song to-morrow.
    Look away! &c.

5

Dar's buck-wheat cakes an' Ingen' batter,
Makes you fat or a little fatter;
    Look away! &c.
Den hoe it down an scratch your grabble,
To Dixie land I'm bound to trabble.
    Look away ! &c.

1860

"J. K."

The Yellow Rose of Texas

There's a yellow rose in Texas that I am going to see,
No other darkey knows her, no darkey only me;
She cried so when I left her, it like to broke my heart,
And if I ever find her we never more will part.

She's the sweetest rose of color this darkey ever knew,
Her eyes are bright as diamonds, they sparkle like the
    dew,
You may talk about your Dearest May, and sing of Rosa
    Lee,
But the yellow rose of Texas beats the belles of
    Tennessee.

2

Where the Rio Grande is flowing, and the starry skies
    are bright,
She walks along the river in the quiet summer night;
She thinks if I remember, when we parted long ago,
I promis'd to come back again, and not to leave her so.

3

Oh! now I'm going to find her, for my heart is full of
    woe,
And we'll sing the song together, that we sung so long
    ago;
We'll play the banjo gaily, and we'll sing the songs of
    yore,
And the yellow rose of Texas shall be mine for evermore.

1858

Kingdom Coming

Say, darkeys, hab you seen de massa,
Wid de muffstash on his face,
Go long de road some time dis mornin',
Like he gwine to leab de place?
He seen a smoke, way up de ribber,
Whar de Linkum gumboats lay;
He took his hat, an' lef berry sudden,
An' I spec he's run away!

CHORUS
De massa run? ha, ha!
De darkey stay? ho, ho!
It mus' be now de kingdom comin',
An de year ob Jubilo!

2

He six foot one way, two foot tudder,
An' he weigh tree hundred pound,
His coat so big, he couldn't pay de tailor,
An' it won't go half way round.
He drill so much dey call him Cap'an,
An' he get so drefful tann'd,
I spec he try an' fool dem Yankees
For to tink he's contraband.

De darkeys feel so lonesome libing
In de log-house on de lawn,
Dey move dar tings to massa's parlor
For to keep it while he's gone.
Dar's wine an' cider in de kitchen,
An' de darkeys dey'll hab some;
I spose dey'll all be cornfiscated
When de Linkum sojers come.

4

De oberseer he make us trouble,
An' he dribe us round a spell;
We lock him up in de smokehouse cellar,
Wid de key trown in de well.
De whip is lost, de han'cuff broken,
But de massa'll hab his pay;
He's ole enough, big enough, ought to known better
Dan to went an' run away.

1862

JAMES A. BLAND

Carry Me Back to Old Virginny

Carry me back to old Virginny,
There's where the cotton and the corn and tatoes grow,
There's where the birds warble sweet in the spring-time,
There's where the old darkey's heart am long'd to go,

There's where I labored so hard for old massa,
Day after day in the field of yellow corn,
No place on earth do I love more sincerely
Than old Virginny, the state where I was born.

Carry me back to old Virginny,
There's where the cotton and the corn and tatoes grow,
There's where the birds warble sweet in the spring-time,
Therc's where this old darkey's heart am long'd to go.

2

Carry me back to old Virginny,
There let me live 'till I wither and decay,
Long by the old Dismal Swamp have I wandered,
There's where this old darkey's life will pass away.
Massa and missis have long gone before me,
Soon we will meet on that bright and golden shore,
There we'll be happy and free from all sorrow,
There's where we'll meet and we'll never part no more.

1878

Oh, Dem Golden Slippers!

Oh, my golden slippers am laid away,
Kase I don't 'spect to wear 'em till my weddin' day,
And my long-tail'd coat, dat I loved so well,
I will wear up in de chariot in de morn;

And my long, white robe dat I bought last June,
I'm gwine to git changed, kase it fits too soon,
And de ole grey hoss dat I used to drive,
I will hitch him to de chariot in de morn.

CHORUS
Oh, dem golden slippers! Oh, dem golden slippers!
Golden slippers I'm gwine to wear, becase dey look so neat;
Oh, dem golden slippers! Oh, dem golden slippers!
Golden slippers Ise gwine to wear,
To walk de golden street.

2

Oh, my ole banjo hangs on de wall,
Kase it aint been tuned since way last fall,
But de darks all say we will hab a good time,
When we ride up in de chariot in de morn;
Dar's ole Brudder Ben and Sister Luce,
Dey will telegraph de news to Uncle Bacco Juice,
What a great camp-meetin' der will be dat day,
When we ride up in de chariot in de morn.

3

So, it's good bye, children, I will have to go
Whar de rain don't fall or de wind don't blow,
And yer ulster coats, why, yer will not need,
When yer ride up in de chariot in de morn;
But yer golden slippers must be nice and clean,
And yer age must be just sweet sixteen,
And yer white kid gloves yer will have to wear,
When yer ride up in de chariot in de morn.

1878

In the Evening by the Moonlight

In de ebening by de moonlight when dis darkies work
   was over,
We would gather round de fire, 'till de hoecake it was
   done.
Den we all would eat our supper, after dat we'd clear de
   kitchen,
Dat's de only time we had to spare, to hab a little fun,
Uncle Gabe would take de fiddle down, dat hung upon
   de wall,
While de silv'ry moon was shining clear and bright,
How de old folks would enjoy it, they would sit all night
   and listen,
As we sang in de ebe'ning by de moonlight.

CHORUS
In de ebening by de moonlight, you could hear us darkies
   singing,
In de ebening by de moonlight you could hear de banjo
   ringing,
How de old folks would enjoy it,
They would sit all night and listen,
As we sang in de ebening by de moonlight.

2

In de ebening by de moonlight when de watchdog
   would be sleeping,
In de corner near de fireplace, beside de ole armchair,
Whar Aunt Chloe used to sit and tell de Piccaninnies
   stories,

And de cabin would be fill'd wid merry coons from near
    and far,
All dem happy times we used to hab, will ne'er return
    again,
Eb'ry thing was den so merry gay and bright,
And I nebber will forget it, when our daily toil was ober,
How we sang in de ebe'ning by de moonlight.

1880

PARLOR BALLADS

Most minstrel songs were originally conceived for men to perform on stage for primarily male audiences. Boys being boys, these songs are often rude even when they aren't racist. Although minstrels frequently performed sentimental ballads, the ultimate audience and arena for such songs were women and their parlors, in which the ladies of the house could play sheet music on their pianos. In an era characterized by what one historian called "the feminization of American culture," nothing could be permitted to violate the propriety of a woman's parlor. "A charm from the skies seems to hallow us there," as the American playwright and librettist John Howard Payne (1791–1852) wrote in "Home! Sweet Home!," his lyric for Englishman Henry Rowley Bishop's 1823 musical play *Clari*. Consequently, even though 19th-century American parlor ballads are frequently more interesting and sophisticated musically than minstrel ditties, the prim gentility of their lyrics often makes them seem vapid on the page, like the "vapor" of Stephen Foster's dream of Jeanie or the "vapors" in "Beautiful Dreamer."

If the words were sometimes pallid, the music was a robust hybrid of English, Scottish, Irish, and Italian sources. Thomas Moore, the Dublin-born poet who set new verses to traditional melodies from Ireland and elsewhere, was the most popular songwriter in the English-speaking world during the first half of the 19th century. Foster published "I Would Not Die in Spring Time" under the pseudonym Milton Moore in semi-homage, and his inspiration for "Ah! May the Red Rose Live Alway!" was clearly Moore's famous song "The Last Rose of Summer."

The *bel canto* operas of Rossini, Bellini, and Donizetti were another influence. Henry Russell, a histrionic English singer and songwriter who toured the States frequently (Foster attended one of his concerts in 1843), claimed to have studied with Rossini and Bellini and unquestionably popularized their legato melodies and rippling triplets (epitomized by "Beautiful Dreamer"). The lyrics to Russell's "Woodman! Spare That Tree!" were penned by George Pope Morris (1802–1864), a prominent New York editor and songwriter. Foster's first copyrighted composition, "Open Thy Lattice Love," set to music other lines by Morris.

During the Civil War, parlor ballads were sung not only by women who missed their menfolk, but also by soldiers on both sides. Lyrics such as those to "Lorena" by Henry DeLafayette Webster (1824–1896) and "Aura Lea" by William Whiteman Fosdick (1825–1862) evoked the many months and miles that separated loved ones and memories that dissolved the distance. (Almost a century later, with other lyrics, "Aura Lea" became the title song of Elvis Presley's first film, *Love Me Tender*.)

Journalist Will S. (for William Shakespeare) Hays (1837–1907) felt an affinity for Foster not only as a fellow songwriter but also because the lifelong Kentuckian wrote a newspaper column for decades about comings and goings on the Ohio River that Foster knew so well. Despite its unpromising title, "I'll Remember You, Love, in My Prayers," particularly its first verse, is among the most vivid of Hays's 322 songs.

"Western Home" strays far from the parlor but not from the genre's veneration of home and, in passages such as "where seldom if ever, / Any poisonous herbage doth grow," its occasionally stilted diction. Although the song did not become well known until the 20th century, when it acquired the title "Home on the Range" and somewhat different words, the original lyric by Brewster Higley (1823–1911) was published in a Kansas newspaper in the early 1870s and soon set to music by Daniel E. Kelley.

Parlors have gone the way of the antimacassars that protected their sofas and chairs, but parlor ballads are still very much with us. Their sentimentality, formality, and tempi live on in songs such as Bob Dylan's "Forever Young," Dolly Parton's "I Will Always Love You," Burt Bacharach and Hal David's "(They Long to Be) Close to You," and Elton John and Bernie Taupin's "Candle in the Wind."

Foster's "Jeanie with the Light Brown Hair" (1854)

STEPHEN C. FOSTER

Ah! May the Red Rose Live Alway!

Ah! may the red rose live alway,
   To smile upon earth and sky!
Why should the beautiful ever weep?
   Why should the beautiful die?
Lending a charm to ev'ry ray
   That falls on her cheeks of light,
Giving the zephyr kiss for kiss,
   And nursing the dewdrop bright—
Ah! may the red rose live alway,
   To smile upon earth and sky!
Why should the beautiful ever weep?
   Why should the beautiful die?

2

Long may the daisies dance the field,
   Frolicking far and near!
Why should the innocent hide their heads?
   Why should the innocent fear?
Spreading their petals in mute delight
   When morn in its radiance breaks,
Keeping a floral festival
   Till the night-loving primrose wakes—
Long may the daisies dance the field,
   Frolicking far and near!
Why should the innocent hide their heads?
   Why should the innocent fear?

Lulled be the dirge in the cypress bough,
  That tells of departed flowers!
Ah! that the butterfly's gilded wing
  Fluttered in evergreen bowers!
Sad is my heart for the blighted plants—
  Its pleasures are aye as brief—
They bloom at the young year's joyful call,
  And fade with the autumn leaf:
Ah! may the red rose live alway,
  To smile upon earth and sky!
Why should the beautiful ever weep?
  Why should the beautiful die?

1850

I Would Not Die in Spring Time

I would not die in Spring time
  When all is bright around,
And fair young flowers are peeping
  From out the silent ground,
When life is on the water
  And joy upon the shore;
For winter, gloomy winter
  Then reigns o'er us no more.

2

I would not die in Summer
  When music's on the breeze,
And soft, delicious murmurs
  Float ever through the trees,

And fairy birds are singing
    From morn till close of day—
No: with its transient glories
    I would not pass away.

3

When breezes leave the mountain,
    Its balmy sweets all o'er—
To breathe around the fountain,
    And fan our bowers no more.
When Summer flowers are dying
    Within the lonely glen,
And Autumn winds are sighing—
    I would not perish then!

4

But let me die in Winter
    When night hangs dark above,
And cold the snow is lying
    On bosoms that we love—
Ah! may the wind at midnight,
    That bloweth from the sea,
Chant mildly, softly, sweetly
    A requiem for me.

1850

Old Dog Tray

The morn of life is past,
And evening comes at last;
It brings me a dream of a once happy day,
Of merry forms I've seen
Upon the village green,
Sporting with my old dog Tray.

CHORUS
Old dog Tray's ever faithful,
Grief cannot drive him away,
He's gentle, he is kind;
I'll never, never find
A better friend than old dog Tray.

2

The forms I call'd my own
Have vanished one by one,
The lov'd ones, the dears ones have all passed away,
Their happy smiles have flown,
Their gentle voices gone;
I've nothing left but old dog Tray.

3

When thoughts recall the past
His eyes are on me cast;
I know that he feels what my breaking heart would say:
Although he cannot speak
I'll vainly, vainly seek
A better friend than old dog Tray.

1853

Jeanie with the Light Brown Hair

I dream of Jeanie with the light brown hair,
Borne, like a vapor, on the summer air;
I see her tripping where the bright streams play,
Happy as the daisies that dance on her way.
Many were the wild notes her merry voice would pour.
Many were the blithe birds that warbled them o'er:
Oh! I dream of Jeanie with the light brown hair,
Floating like a vapor, on the soft summer air.

2

I long for Jeanie with the day-dawn smile,
Radiant in gladness, warm with winning guile;
I hear her melodies, like joys gone by,
Sighing round my heart o'er the fond hopes that die:
Sighing like the night wind and sobbing like the rain,
Wailing for the lost one that comes not again:
Oh! I long for Jeanie, and my heart bows low,
Never more to find her where the bright waters flow.

3

I sigh for Jeanie, but her light form strayed
Far from the fond hearts round her native glade;
Her smiles have vanished and her sweet song flown,
Flitting like the dreams that have cheered us and gone.
Now the nodding wild flowers may wither on the shore
While her gentle fingers will cull them no more:
Oh! I sigh for Jeanie with the light brown hair,
Floating, like a vapor, on the soft summer air.

1854

Gentle Annie

Thou wilt come no more, gentle Annie,
Like a flower thy spirit did depart;
Thou art gone, alas! like the many
That have bloomed in the summer of my heart.

CHORUS
Shall we never more behold thee;
Never hear thy winning voice again
When the Springtime comes, gentle Annie,
When the wild flowers are scattered o'er the plain?

2

We have roamed and loved mid the bowers
When thy downy cheeks were in their bloom;
Now I stand alone mid the flowers
While they mingle their perfumes o'er thy tomb.

3

Ah! the hours grow sad while I ponder
Near the silent spot where thou art laid,
And my heart bows down when I wander
By the streams and the meadows where we strayed.

1856

Linger in Blissful Repose

Linger in blissful repose,
Free from all sorrowing care love,
While round thee melody flows,
Wafted on pinions of air love.
Let not thy visions depart,
Lured by the stars that are beaming,
Music will flow from my heart
While thy sweet spirit is dreaming.
Dreaming, dreaming, unfettered by the day,
In melody, in melody I'll breathe I'll breathe my soul
    away.

2

Softly the night winds are heard,
Sighing o'er mountain and dale, love,
Gently the vapors are stirred
Down in the shadowy vale love.
While o'er the dew covered plain,
Starlight in silence is gleaming,
Lightly I'll breathe a refrain
Round the young heart that is dreaming.
Dreaming, dreaming, unfettered by the day,
In melody, in melody I'll breathe I'll breathe my soul
    away.

1858

Beautiful Dreamer

Beautiful dreamer, wake unto me,
Starlight and dewdrops are waiting for thee;
Sounds of the rude world heard in the day,
Lull'd by the moonlight have all pass'd away!
Beautiful dreamer, queen of my song,
List while I woo thee with soft melody;
Gone are the cares of life's busy throng,
Beautiful dreamer, awake unto me!
Beautiful dreamer, awake unto me!

2

Beautiful dreamer, out on the sea
Mermaids are chanting the wild lorelie;
Over the streamlet vapors are borne,
Waiting to fade at the bright coming morn.
Beautiful dreamer, beam on my heart,
E'en as the morn on the streamlet and sea;
Then will all clouds of sorrow depart,
Beautiful dreamer, awake unto me!
Beautiful dreamer, awake unto me!

1864

Kiss Me Dear Mother Ere I Die

Bend o'er my pillow my mother dear
Life's chilling close is now drawing near
Drive from about me these clouds of fear
Breathe o'er my brow a parting sigh,

I have been wayward unto thee
Now I can feel it painfully
Patient and kind wert thou to me
Kiss me dear mother ere I die.

2

Tell me of angels that dwell above
Then from my heart will the tear drops move
Whisper to me gentle words of love
While I in gloom and suff'ring lie,
I have been wayward unto thee
Now I can feel it painfully
Patient and kind wert thou to me
Kiss me dear mother ere I die.

1869

JOHN HOWARD PAYNE

(*Henry R. Bishop, music*)

Home! Sweet Home!

'Mid pleasures and palaces though we may roam,
Be it ever so humble there's no place like home!
A charm from the skies seems to hallow us there,
Which seek through the world, is ne'er met with
        elsewhere:
    Home! Home! sweet, sweet Home!
    There's no place like Home!
    There's no place like Home!

An exile from Home, splendour dazzles in vain,
Oh! give me my lowly thatch'd cottage again!
The birds singing gaily that came at my call,
Give me them with the peace of mind dearer than all:
    Home! Home! sweet, sweet Home!
    There's no place like Home!
    There's no place like Home!

1823

GEORGE POPE MORRIS

(*Henry Russell, music*)

Woodman! Spare That Tree!

Woodman spare that tree!
    Touch not a single bough;
In youth it sheltered me,
    And I'll protect it now;
'Twas my forefather's hand
    That placed it near his cot,
There, woodman, let it stand,
    Thy axe shall harm it not!

That old familiar tree,
    Whose glory and renown
Are spread o'er land and sea,
    And wouldst thou hack it down?
Woodman, forbear thy stroke!
    Cut not its earth-bound ties;
Oh! spare that aged oak,
    Now towering to the skies!

When but an idle boy
    I sought its grateful shade;
In all their gushing joy
    Here, too, my sisters played.
My mother kiss'd me here;
    My father press'd my hand—
Forgive this foolish tear,
    But let that old oak stand!

My heart-strings round thee cling,
    Close as thy bark, old friend!
Here shall the wild-bird sing,
    And still thy branches bend.
Old tree! the storm still brave!
    And, woodman, leave the spot;
While I've a hand to save,
    Thy axe shall harm it not.

1838

HENRY D. L. WEBSTER

(*J. P. Webster, music*)

Lorena

The years creep slowly by, Lorena,
    The snow is on the grass again;
The sun's low down the sky, Lorena,
    The frost gleams where the flow'rs have been.

But the heart throbs on as warmly now,
  As when the summer days were nigh;
Oh! the sun can never dip so low,
  Adown affection's cloudless sky.
The sun can never dip so low,
  Adown affection's cloudless sky.

2

A hundred months have passed Lorena,
  Since last I held that hand in mine,
And felt the pulse beat fast, Lorena,
  Though mine beat faster far than thine.
A hundred months,—'twas flowery May
  When up the hilly slope we climbed
To watch the dying of the day,
  And hear the distant church bells chimed.
To watch the dying of the day,
  And hear the distant church bells chimed.

3

We loved each other then, Lorena,
  More than we ever dared to tell;
And what we might have been, Lorena,
  Had but our lovings prospered well—
But then, 'tis past—the years are gone,
  I'll not call up their shadowy forms;
I'll say to them, "lost years, sleep on!
  Sleep on! nor heed, life's pelting storm."
I'll say to them, "lost years, sleep on!
  Sleep on! nor heed, life's pelting storm."

4

The story of that past, Lorena,
    Alas! I care not to repeat,
The hopes that could not last, Lorena,
    They lived, but only lived to cheat.
I would not cause e'en one regret
    To wrankle in your bosom now;
For "if we *try*, we may forget,"
    Were words of thine long years ago.
For "if we *try*, we may forget,"
    Were words of thine long years ago.

5

Yes, these were words of thine, Lorena,
    They burn within my memory yet;
They touched some tender chords, Lorena,
    Which thrill and tremble with regret.
'Twas not thy woman's heart that spoke;
    Thy heart was always true to me:—
A *duty* stern and pressing, broke
    The tie which linked my soul with thee.
A *duty* stern and pressing, broke
    The tie which linked my soul with thee.

6

It matters little now, Lorena,
    The past—is in the eternal Past,
Our heads will soon lie low, Lorena,
    Life's tide is ebbing out so fast.
There is a Future! O thank God,
    Of life *this* is so small a part;

'Tis dust to dust beneath the sod;
    But there, *up there*, 'tis heart to heart.
'Tis dust to dust beneath the sod;
    But there, *up there*, 'tis heart to heart.

1857

W. W. FOSDICK

(*George R. Poulton, music*)

Aura Lea

When the Blackbird in the Spring,
    On the willow tree
Sat and rock'd,
    I heard him sing,
Singing Aura Lea.
    Aura Lea, Aura Lea,
Maid of golden hair;
    Sunshine came along with thee,
And swallows in the air.

CHORUS
Aura Lea, Aura Lea,
    Maid of golden hair;
Sunshine came along with thee,
    And swallows in the air.

2

In thy blush the rose was born,
   Music, when you spake,
Through thine azure eye the morn,
   Sparkling, seemed to break.
Aura Lea, Aura Lea,
   Birds of crimson wing
Never song have sung to me
   As in that sweet spring.

3

Aura Lea! the bird may flee,
   The willow's golden hair,
Swing through winter fitfully,
   On the stormy air.
Yet if thy blue eyes I see,
   Gloom will soon depart;
For to me, sweet Aura Lea
   Is sunshine through the heart.

4

When the mistletoe was green,
   Midst the winter's snows,
Sunshine in thy face was seen,
   Kissing lips of rose.
Aura Lea, Aura Lea,
   Take my golden ring;
Love and light return with thee,
   And swallows with the spring.

1861

I'll Remember You, Love, in My Prayers

When the curtains of night are pinned back by the stars,
    And the beautiful moon leaps the skies,
And the dewdrops of Heaven are kissing the rose,
    It is then that my memory flies,
As if on the wings of some beautiful dove,
    In haste with the message it bears
To bring you a kiss of affection and say,
    "I remember you, love, in my prayers"

CHORUS
Go where you will—on land or at sea—
    I'll share all your sorrows and cares;
And at night, when I kneel by my bedside and pray,
    I'll remember you, love, in my prayers.

I have loved you too fondly to ever forget
    The love you have spoken for me,
And the kiss of affection still warm on my lips
    When you told me how true you would be.
I know not if Fortune be fickle or friend,
    Or if time on your memory wears;
I know that I love you wherever you roam,
    And remember you, love, in my prayers.

When heavenly angels are guarding the good,
　　As God has ordain'd them to do,
In answer to prayers I have offered to Him,
　　I know there is one watching you;
And may its bright spirit be with you through life
　　To guide you up Heaven's bright stairs,
And meet with the one who has loved you so true,
　　And remembered you, love, in her prayers.

1895; first published 1869

BREWSTER HIGLEY

(*Daniel E. Kelley, music*)

Western Home

Oh! give me a home where the buffalo roam,
Where the deer and the antelope play;
Where never is heard a discouraging word,
And the sky is not clouded all day.

CHORUS
A home! A home!
Where the deer and antelope play,
Where seldom is heard a discouraging word,
And the sky is not clouded all day.

Oh! give me a land where the bright diamond sand
Throws its light from the glittering streams,
Where glideth along the graceful white swan,
Like the maid in her heavenly dreams.

3

Oh! give me a gale of the Solomon vale,
Where the life streams with buoyancy flow;
Or the banks of the Beaver, where seldom if ever,
Any poisonous herbage doth grow.

4

How often at night, when the heavens were bright
With the light of the twinkling stars,
Have I stood here amazed, and asked as I gazed,
If their glory exceed that of ours.

5

I love the wild flowers in this bright land of ours;
I love the wild curlew's shrill scream;
The bluffs and white rocks, and antelope flocks
That gaze on the mountains so green.

6

The air is so pure and the breeze so free,
The zephyrs so balmy and light,
That I would not exchange my home here to range
Forever in azures so bright.

1876; written 1872 or 1873

HENRY CLAY WORK

Grandfather's Clock

My grandfather's clock was too large for the shelf,—
So it stood ninety years on the floor;
It was taller by half than the old man himself,
Though it weighed not a pennyweight more.
It was bought on the morn of the day that he was born,
And was always his treasure and pride;
But it stopp'd short—never to go again—
When the old man died.

CHORUS
Ninety years, without slumbering (tick, tick, tick, tick),
His life seconds numbering (tick, tick, tick, tick),
It stopp'd short—never to go again—
When the old man died.

2

In watching its pendulum swing to and fro,
Many hours had he spent while a boy;
And in childhood and manhood the clock seemed to know
And to share both his grief and his joy.
For it struck twenty-four when he entered at the door,
With a blooming and beautiful bride;
But it stopp'd short—never to go again—
When the old man died.

3

My grandfather said that of those he could hire,
Not a servant so faithful he found;
For it wasted no time, and had but one desire—
At the close of each week to be wound.
And it kept in its place—not a frown upon its face,
And its hands never hung by its side;
But it stopp'd short—never to go again—
When the old man died.

4

It rang an alarm in the dead of the night—
An alarm that for years had been dumb;
And we knew that his spirit was pluming for flight—
That his hour of departure had come.
Still the clock kept time, with a soft and muffled chime,
As we silently stood by his side;
But it stopp'd short—never to go again—
When the old man died.

1876

DRINKING AND
TEMPERANCE SONGS

Stephen Foster's life, like the American experience, was steeped in alcohol. Our national anthem is set to the melody of an English drinking song. Pittsburgh was the epicenter of the Whiskey Rebellion. Alcohol likely contributed to the financial setbacks of Foster's father, and certainly to Foster's own monetary and marital difficulties as well as to his death.

Temperance was an extraordinarily powerful social movement before (not to mention after) the Civil War, claiming many more adherents than abolition could muster. Foster's father joined the Pittsburgh Temperance Society in 1833 and millions of followers of the Washingtonian movement soon after it was founded in a Baltimore tavern in 1840. Probably to the mortification of his family, William Foster publicly proclaimed himself a reformed drunkard at Washingtonian conventions. Even more mortifying, he may have fallen off the wagon subsequently.

Although Stephen Foster does not spell out in "Willie We Have Missed You" the cause(s) of Willie's absence, by the time it was published he had probably taken to the bottle and he had definitely experienced the first of several separations from his wife. The same year, 1854, saw the publication of Timothy Shay Arthur's cautionary tract *Ten Nights in a Barroom*, in which one of alcohol's many victims is the gifted wastrel Willy Hammond. (When *Ten Nights* was turned into a stage melodrama in 1858, one of its highlights was Henry Clay Work's "Come Home, Father!")

Foster published his first song explicitly about drinking, "Comrades Fill No Glass for Me," in 1855.

Foster was too compromised to crusade for temperance like the teetotaling Hutchinson Family Singers. Various permutations of these 13 siblings from Milford, New Hampshire, were one of America's most popular vocal groups before the Civil War. Accompanying their four-part harmonies with violin and cello, the Hutchinsons performed in concert and at rallies and conventions across the country. Embracing abolition as well as temperance, they were earnest, engaged folk and protest singers more than a century before the Weavers and Peter, Paul, and Mary performed an updated version of the Hutchinsons' "If I Were a Voice," retitled "If I Had a Hammer."

The Hutchinson Family Singers frequently wrote provocative new lyrics for familiar tunes that audiences could easily sing. Set to a traditional melody, "King Alcohol" was published in 1843 as "a Comic Temperance Glee," but it's a deadly serious temperance anthem proclaiming, "The shout of Washingtonians is heard on every gale."

The attitude toward alcohol is more tolerant though no less telling in later temperance songs such as "The Little Brown Jug," the only major hit composed by Joseph Eastburn Winter (1837–1918), the younger brother of the more famous Philadelphia songwriter Septimus Winner (see page 143), and "I'll Never Get Drunk Any More," words by Edward Harrigan (1844–1911) and music by David Braham, the most successful composers of musical comedies from the 1870s to the 1890s (see page 81).

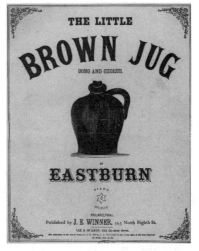

Foster's "Comrades, Fill No Glass for Me" (1855) and Joseph Eastburn Winner's "The Little Brown Jug" (1869)

STEPHEN C. FOSTER

Willie We Have Missed You

Oh! Willie, is it you, dear,
Safe, safe at home?
They did not tell me true, dear;
They said you would not come.
I heard you at the gate,
And it made my heart rejoice;
For I knew that welcome footstep
And that dear, familiar voice,
Making music on my ear
In the lonely midnight gloom:
Oh! Willie, we have missed you;
Welcome, welcome home!

2

We've longed to see you nightly,
But this night of all;
The fire was blazing brightly
And lights were in the hall.
The little ones were up
Till 'twas ten o'clock and past,
Then their eyes began to twinkle,
And they've gone to sleep at last;
But they listened for your voice
Till they thought you'd never come;
Oh! Willie, we have missed you;
Welcome, welcome home!

The days were sad without you,
The nights long and drear;
My dreams have been about you;
Oh! welcome, Willie dear!
Last night I wept and watched
By the moonlight's cheerless ray,
Till I thought I heard your footstep,
Then I wiped my tears away;
But my heart grew sad again
When I found you had not come;
Oh! Willie, we have missed you;
Welcome, welcome home!

1854

Comrades Fill No Glass for Me

Oh! comrades, fill no glass for me
   To drown my soul in liquid flame,
For if I drank, the toast should be
   To blighted fortune, health and fame.
Yet, though I long to quell the strife,
That passion holds against my life,
Still, boon companions may ye be,
But comrades, fill no glass for me.

2

I know a breast that once was light
   Whose patient sufferings need my care,
I know a hearth that once was bright,
   But drooping hopes have nestled there.

Then while the tear drops nightly steal
From the wounded hearts that I should heal,
Though boon companions ye may be—
Oh! comrades, fill no glass for me.

3

When I was young I felt the tide
   Of aspirations undefiled,
But manhood's years have wronged the pride
   My parents centered in their child.
Then, by a mother's sacred tear,
By all that memory should revere,
Though boon companions ye may be—
Oh! comrades, fill no glass for me.

1855

The Wife

He'll come home, he'll not forget me, for his word is
      always true.
He's gone to sup
The deadly cup,
And while the long night through,
He's gone to quaff,
And talk and laugh
To while the drear night through:
He'll come home, he'll not forget me, for his word is
      always true.

2

He'll come home with tears and pleading words and ask
    me to forget.
Can I be his
While he is mine
And cause him one regret?
My heart may break,
But for his sake
I'll do all I can do.
He'll come home, he'll not forget me, for his word is
    always true.

3

He'll come home with sorrow on his heart that none but
    he can know
With pangs of thought,
How dearly bought!
And fears of coming woe;
He'll feel the cost
Of days now lost
That time can ne'er renew.
He'll come home, he'll not forget me, for his word is
    always true.

1860

JESSE HUTCHINSON JR.

King Alcohol

King Alcohol has many forms
   By which he catches men.
He is a beast of many horns
   And ever thus has been.

CHORUS (1 & 2)
For there's rum, and gin, and beer, and wine
   And brandy of logwood hue
And hock, and port, and flip combine
   To make a man look blue
He says be merry, for here's good sherry
And Tom and Jerry, Champagne and Perry,
   And spirits of every hue,
O are these not a fiendish crew
   As ever a mortal knew.
O are not these not a fiendish crew
   As ever a mortal knew

   2

King Alcohol is very sly
   A liar from the first.
He'll make you drink until you're dry
   Then drink, because you thirst.

3

King Alcohol has had his day
   His kingdom's crumbling fast
His votaries are heard to say
   Our tumbling days are past.

CHORUS (3 & 4)
For there's no rum, nor gin, nor beer, nor wine
   Nor brandy of any hue
Nor hock, nor port, nor flip combined
   To make a man get blue
And now they're merry, without their sherry
Or Tom or Jerry, champagne and perry
   Or spirits of every hue.
And now they are a temperate crew
   As ever a mortal knew
And now they are a temperate crew
   And have given the devil his due.

4

The shout of Washingtonians
   Is heard on every gale
They're chanting now the victory
   O'er cider, beer, and ale.

1843

HENRY CLAY WORK

"Come Home, Father!"

'Tis the Song of Little Mary,
Standing at the bar-room door,
While the shameful midnight revel
Rages wildly as before.

Father, dear father, come home with me now!
The clock in the steeple strikes one;
You said you were coming right home from the shop,
As soon as your day's work was done.
Our fire has gone out—our house is all dark—
And mother's been watching since tea,
With poor brother Benny so sick in her arms,
And no one to help her but me.
Come home! come home! come home!
Please, father, *dear* father, come home.

CHORUS
Hear the sweet voice of the child,
Which the night-winds repeat as they roam!
Oh who could resist this most plaintive of prayers?
"Please, father, dear father, come home!"

2

Father, dear father, come home with me now!
The clock in the steeple strikes two;
The night has grown colder, and Benny is worse—
But he has been calling for you.
Indeed he is worse—Ma says he will die,

Perhaps before morning shall dawn;
And this is the message she sent me to bring—
"Come quickly, or he will be gone."
Come home! come home! come home!
Please, father, *dear* father, come home.

3

Father, dear father, come home with me now!
The clock in the steeple strikes three;
The house is so lonely—the hours are so long
For poor weeping mother and me.
Yes, we are alone—poor Benny is dead,
And gone with the angels of light;
And these were the very last words that he said—
"I want to kiss Papa good night."
Come home! come home ! come home!
Please, father, *dear* father, come home.

1864

JOSEPH EASTBURN WINNER

The Little Brown Jug

My wife and I lived all alone,
    In a little log hut we called our own;
She loved gin and I loved rum,—
    I tell you what, we'd lots of fun.

Ha, ha, ha, you and me,
   "Little brown jug" don't I love thee;
Ha, ha, ha, you and me,
   "Little brown jug" don't I love thee.

2

'Tis you who makes my friends my foes,
   'Tis you who makes me wear old clothes;
Here you are, so near my nose,
   So tip her up, and down she goes.

3

When I go toiling to my farm,
   I take little "Brown Jug" under my arm;
I place it under a shady tree,
   Little "Brown Jug" 'tis you and me.

4

If all the folks in Adam's race,
   Were gathered together in one place;
Then I'd prepare to shed a tear,
   Before I'd part from you, my dear.

5

If I'd a cow that gave such milk
   I'd clothe her in the finest silk;
I'd feed her on the choicest hay,
   And milk her forty times a day.

6

The rose is red, my nose is, too,
   The violet's blue, and so are you;
And yet I guess before I stop,
   We'd better take another drop.

1869

EDWARD HARRIGAN

(*David Braham, music*)

I'll Never Get Drunk Any More

I remember when a bit of a boy,
   The lesson they taught at home,
If I wanted to be a great man
   I must leave the liquor alone.
My father was a great drinker
   He never was sober a day
And when he'd roll in, in the morning
   Oh these are the words he would say.

CHORUS
I'll never get drunk any more,
I'll never get drunk any more.
The pledge I will take, thc whiskey I'll shake,
Oh, I'll never get drunk any more.

2

Well of course you know I took after my dad
  And I got so I'd take a wee drop
But a little it goes a great way
  It's the divel's own job for to stop
Whin I married my wife I was sober
  I drank nothing but coffee and tay
I was drunk the night of the wedding
  Thin to her these words I did say.

3

Whinever I get a dose of the blues
  I sind for a bottle and bowl
Of the rale ould stuff in the closet
  Thin into me bed shure I roll,
When I wake me head it is swimmin
  Pulverized wid the liquor I lay,
Then I take a cocktail in the morning
  And these are the words that I say.

4

If I had the pluck of N-ap-ole-le-on
  Wid the good since of General Grant
Like a sober old judge I'd lave off the budge
  On my word and my honor I cant—
You might try for to take Giberalter
  And talk till my hair it was gray,
And when I lay down in me coffin
  These are the words that I say.

1874

SONGS OF PROTEST
AND POVERTY

Although his plantation melodies frequently expressed sympathy for the plight of slaves, Foster published scarcely any songs of political protest. "Hard Times Come Again No More" is a striking exception that has been recorded more frequently in recent years than any other Foster composition. It was probably inspired by widespread economic distress in 1854 and by Charles Dickens' recently serialized novel *Hard Times*, set in an imaginary Coketown —"a town of machinery and tall chimneys, out of which interminable serpents of smoke trailed themselves forever and ever"—that may have reminded Foster of Pittsburgh. In his declining days, which Foster eerily anticipated in the lurid "The Little Ballad Girl," he was reported to have sung "Hard Times" "with a pathos that a state of semi-inebriation often lends the voice."

One of Foster's closest friends, Charles Shiras (1824–1854), was more politically engaged and an outspoken abolitionist. The Hutchinson Family Singers adapted and set to music one of Shiras' poems, "The Popular Credo," renaming it "The Popular Creed." The Hutchinsons adapted another poem, "A Hundred Years Hence," by the pioneering abolitionist and feminist Frances Dana Barker Gage (1808–1884), whose high hopes for the future have been so thoroughly dashed that one doesn't know whether to snicker or cry—or both. Jesse Hutchinson Jr. (1813–1853) wrote the words as well the music for "Eight Dollars a Day," which suggests how little has changed in more than a century and a half (the war the craven congressmen support is President James K. Polk's against Mexico). He also composed new lyrics for the abolitionist rallying cry "Get Off the Track!," combining calculation and irony when he appropriated for the song's melody that of the minstrel ditty "Old Dan Tucker" (see p. 34). Why should the Devil have all the good tunes? "Darling Nelly Gray" is another illustration of the knotty ties between minstrelsy and abolitionism. Its author, Benjamin Hanby (1833–1867), an Ohio schoolteacher, minister, and songwriter, made explicit the antislavery sentiment of Foster's "My Old Kentucky Home" and rid it of racial epithets even as he otherwise echoed its language. Four years later, Foster in turn echoed Hanby's "I'm coming—coming—coming, as the angels clear the way" in the chorus of "Old Black Joe."

Solon Robinson (1803–1880), a prominent authority on agriculture, occasionally ventured down New York's meaner streets for Horace Greeley's *New York Tribune*. One of his stories spawned "The Dying Words of Little Katy; or Will He Come." Katy, peddling roasted ears of corn, is a tear-jerking cousin of "The Little Ballad Girl" and may have inspired Foster's song.

More than their comedy made Edward Harrigan and David Braham's musicals about life among the immigrants (and African Americans) teeming on New York City's Lower East Side crowd pleasers for decades. Audiences appreciated Harrigan's expressions of solidarity with the working class ("No Wealth Without Labor") and of sympathy for the oppressed, as when "McNally's Rows of Flats" equates the political, economic, and racial exploitation of slum housing with a previous American "peculiar institution": slavery. Harrigan and Braham, incidentally, interpolated a verse from Foster's "Hard Times" into the chorus of another of their songs.

The Hutchinson Family Singers (c. 1843)

Hard Times Come Again No More

Let us pause in life's pleasures and count its many tears
   While we all sup sorrow with the poor:
There's a song that will linger forever in our ears;
   Oh! Hard Times, come again no more.

CHORUS
'Tis the song the sigh of the weary;
Hard Times, Hard Times, come again no more;
Many days you have lingered around my cabin door,
Oh! Hard Times, come again no more.

2

While we seek mirth and beauty and music light and gay
   There are frail forms fainting at the door:
Though their voices are silent, their pleading looks will
    say
   Oh! Hard Times, come again no more.

3

There's a pale drooping maiden who toils her life away
   With a worn heart whose better days are o'er:
Though her voice would be merry, 'tis sighing all the
    day
   Oh! Hard Times, come again no more.

'Tis a sigh that is wafted across the troubled wave,
　'Tis a wail that is heard upon the shore,
'Tis a dirge that is murmured around the lowly grave,
　Oh! Hard Times, come again no more.

1854

The Little Ballad Girl

Ho! little girl, so dressed with care!
With fairy slippers and golden hair!
What did I hear you calling so loud,
Down in that heartless, motley crowd?

CHORUS
　'Tis my father's song
　And he can't live long;
Everyone knows he wrote it,
　For I've been down at the hotel door,
And all the gentlemen bought it.

2

Ho! little girl, let me light my cigar!
Where are you going tonight so far?
What are you hiding under your arm?
If I burn a sheet, will it do any harm?

3

Ho! little girl, what makes you cry?
Come, dry up the tears in that bright blue eye!
What is all this that is blowing around,
All soiled and scattered and strewn on the ground.

1860

JESSE HUTCHINSON JR.

Get Off the Track!

Ho! the Car Emancipation
Rides majestic thro' our nation
Bearing on its Train the story,
LIBERTY! a Nation's Glory
    Roll it along, thro' the Nation
    Freedom's Car, Emancipation.

2

First of all the train, and greater
Speeds the dauntless *Liberator*
Onward cheered amid hosannas,
And the waving of Free Banners.
    Roll it along! spread your Banners
    While the people shout hosannas.

3

Men of various predilections,
Frightened, run in all directions;
Merchants, Editors, Physicians,
Lawyers, Priests and Politicians.
    Get out of the way! every station,
    Clear the track of 'mancipation.

4

Let the Ministers and Churches
Leave behind sectarian lurches;
Jump on board the Car of Freedom
Ere it be too late to need them.
 Sound the alarm! Pulpit's thunder!
 Ere too late, you see your blunder.

5

Politicians gazed, astounded,
When, at first our Bell resounded;
Freight trains are coming, tell these Foxes,
With our *Votes* and *Ballot Boxes*,
 Jump for your lives! Politicians,
 From your dangerous false positions.

6

Rail Roads to Emancipation
Cannot rest on *Clay* foundation
And the *tracks* of *"The Magician"*
Are but *Rail Roads* to perdition.
 Pull up the Rails! Emancipation
 Cannot rest on such foundation.

7

All true friends of Emancipation,
Haste to Freedom's Rail Road Station;
Quick into the Cars get seated,
All is ready, and completed.
 Put on the Steam! All are crying,
 And the Liberty Flags are flying.

8

Now, again the Bell is tolling,
Soon you'll see the car wheels rolling;
Hinder not their destination,
Chartered for Emancipation.
 Wood up the fire! keep it flashing,
 While the Train goes onward dashing.

9

Hear the mighty car wheels humming!
Now look out! *The Engine's coming!*
Church and Statesman! hear the thunder!
Clear the track! or you'll fall under.
 Get off the track! all are singing,
 While the *Liberty Bell* is ringing.

10

On triumphant, see them bearing,
Through sectarian rubbish tearing;
Th' Bell and Whistle and the Steaming,
Startles thousands from their dreaming.
 Look out for the cars! while the Bell rings,
 Ere the sound your funeral knell rings.

11

See the people run to meet us;
At the Depots thousands greet us;
All take seats with exultation,
In the Car Emancipation.
 Huzza! Huzza! Emancipation
 Soon will bless our happy nation.
  Huzza! . . . Huzza!! . . . Huzza!!! . . .

1844

Eight Dollars a Day

(*J. J. Hutchinson, music*)

At Washington, full once a year do politicians throng
Contriving there by various arts to make their sessions
     long;
And many a reason do they give why they're obliged to
     stay,
But the clearest reason yet adduced is Eight dollars a day

2

Just go with me to the Capitol, if you really would behold
All that imagination craves, and more than e'er was told;
D'ye see the City av'nue swarms with members grave
     and gay
And what d'ye s'pose they're thinking of! 'tis Eight
     dollars a day.

3

There is an axiom known to all and rather old given
For 'tis a common household phrase and very often seen;
That those who're fools enough to dance the fiddler too
     must pay
So Congress fiddles us the tune—of Eight dollars a day.

4

All Washington now is wide awake, and all the big hotels
Are fill'd with Representatives, and O! how liquor sells;
It cannot well be otherwise for think you men will play
The National tune without their grog—of Eight dollars
     a day.

5

A startling scene will now be play'd before the gazing
world
For from the nation's Capitol her banner is unfurl'd;
The Congress men are trudging on, each in his chosen
way
And all keep time to the glorious tune of Eight dollars a
day.

6

Now to the Senate chamber first, then to the House
we'll go
And learn a lesson while we may of patriotic throe;
The roll is called and quorum form'd when the
Chaplains rise to pray
And then the National work begins at Eight dollars a day.

7

Then every member takes his seat in the velvet chair of
state
Thinking that in his dignity's embodied the nation's fate;
A flaming speech is made by one when the call is yea or
nay
But all are agreed when the question comes of Eight
dollars a day.

8

And next in the order of the day comes the mad cry of war.
While very few of the longest heads can hardly tell
what's for
But "War exists" all parties cry and th'enemy we must
slay
So Congress backs the President,—at Eight dollars a day.

9

Then the cry of war runs through the land for Volunteers to go,
And fight in the war for slavery on the plains of Mexico;
Seven dollars a month and to be shot at that is common
soldiers' pay.
While those who send the poor fellows there get Eight
dollars a day.

10

Thus ring our Legislative halls from year to year the
same
Tariffs and Banks and Treasury acts and glorious deeds
of fame;
Our country's great and rich withal, and must be taxed
to pay
And Uncle Sam must foot the bills at Eight dollars a day.

11

But a day of reck'ning's coming on behold the gath'ring
storm
For the People are the Sovereigns yet, and they demand
reform;
From North and South the shout is heard and Congress
must obey
Or quit their seats for better men, at Eight dollars a day.

1848

CHARLES P. SHIRAS

(*The Hutchinson Family Singers, music*)

The Popular Creed

Dimes and dollars! Dollars and dimes!
An empty pocket's the worst of crimes!
If a man's down, give him a thrust!
Trample the beggar into the dust!
Presumptuous poverty, quite appalling!
Knock him over! Kick him for falling!
If a man's up, oh, lift him higher!
Your soul's for sale, and he's a buyer!
Dimes and dollars! Dollars and dimes!
An empty pocket's the worst of crimes!

I know a poor but a worthy youth,
Whose hopes are built on a maiden's truth;
But the maiden will break her vows with ease,
For a wooer cometh whose charms are these:
A hollow heart and an empty head,
A face well tinged with the brandy's red,
A soul well trained in villainy's school,
And cash, sweet cash!—he knoweth the rule.
Dimes and dollars! Dollars and dimes!
An empty pocket's the worst of crimes!

I know a bold and an honest man,
Who strives to live on the Christian plan.
He struggles against a fearful odds—

Who will not bow to the people's gods?
Dimes and dollars! Dollars and dimes!
An empty pocket's the worst of crimes!
So get ye wealth, no matter how!
No question's asked of the rich, I trow!
Steal by night, and steal by day
(Doing it all in a legal way!)
Dimes and dollars! dollars and dimes
An empty pocket's the worst of crimes!

1853

FRANCES D. GAGE

(*The Hutchinson Family Singers, music*)

A Hundred Years Hence

One hundred years hence, what a change will be made,
In politics, morals, religion and trade,
In statesmen who wrangle or ride on the fence,
These things will be altered *a hundred years hence*.

Our laws then will be uncompulsory rules,
Our prisons converted to national schools,
The pleasure of sinning 'tis all a pretense,
And the people will find it so, *a hundred years hence*.

Lying, cheating and fraud will be laid on the shelf,
Men will neither get drunk, nor be bound up in self,
But all live together, good neighbors and friends,
Just as *Christian folks* ought to, *a hundred years hence*.

Then woman, man's partner, man's equal shall stand,
While beauty and harmony govern the land,
To think for oneself will be no offense,
The world will be thinking *a hundred years hence*.

Oppression and war will be heard of no more,
Nor the blood of a slave leave his print on our shore,
Conventions will then be a useless expense,
For we'll all go *free-suffrage a hundred years hence*.

Instead of speech-making to satisfy wrong,
All will join the glad chorus to sing Freedom's song;
And if the Millenium is not a pretense,
We'll all be good brothers *a hundred years hence*.

1886; written 1852

SOLON ROBINSON

(*Horace Waters, music*)

The Dying Words of Little Katy, or Will He Come

Here's hot corn, nice hot corn, a voice was crying!
Sweet hot corn, sweet hot corn, the breeze was sighing!
Come buy, come buy, the world's unfeeling—
How can she sell while sleep is stealing?

CHORUS
Hot corn! Hot corn! *do* buy my nice hot corn.
Hot corn! Hot corn! *do* buy my nice hot corn.

2

All alone, all alone, she sat there weeping;
While at home, while at home, her sister's sleeping.
Come buy, come buy, I'm tired of staying;
Come buy, come buy, I'm tired of saying—
  Hot corn, come buy my nice hot corn.

3

Often there, often there, she sat so drear'ly
With one thought, for she lov'd her sister dearly,
Didst hate? didst hate? how could she ever?
How could she hate her mother? never!
  Hot corn, come buy my nice hot corn.

4

Often there, often there, while others playing,
Hear the cry, buy my corn, she's ever praying,
Pray buy, pray buy, kind hearted stranger,
One ear, then home, I'll brave the danger.
    Hot corn, come buy my nice hot corn.

5

Now at home, now at home, her cry is changing!
Will he come? will he come? while fever's raging
She cries, she cries, pray let me see him.
Once more, once more, pray let me see him.
    Hot corn, he'll buy my nice hot corn.

6

Will he come? will he come? she's constant crying,
Will he come? will he come? poor Katy's dying.
'Twas he! 'twas he! kind words was speaking
Hot corn, hot corn, while I was seeking
    Hot corn, who'll buy my nice hot corn?

7

Midnight there, midnight there, my hot corn crying,
Kindly spoke, first kind words, they stopt my sighing,
That night, that night, when sleep was stealing,
Kind words, kind words, my heart was healing.
    Hot corn, he'll buy my nice hot corn!

8

Will he come? will he come?—weak hands are feeling!
He has come! he has come !—I see him kneeling—

One kiss—the light—how dim 'tis growing—
I thank—'tis dark—good bye—I'm going—
    Hot corn—no more shall cry—hot corn!!!

9

Drop a tear, drop a tear, for she's departed,
Drop a tear, drop a tear, poor broken hearted;
A pledge—a pledge—the world is crying,
Take warning—warning—by Katy's dying.
    Hot corn, who'll buy my nice hot corn?

1853

BENJAMIN HANBY

Darling Nelly Gray

There's a low green valley on the old Kentucky shore,
   There I've whiled many happy hours away,
A sitting and a singing by the little cottage door
   Where lived my darling Nelly Gray.

CHORUS
Oh! my poor Nelly Gray, they have taken you away
   And I'll never see my darling any more,
I'm sitting by the river and I'm weeping all the day,
   For you've gone from the old Kentucky shore.

2

When the moon had climb'd the mountain and the stars
    were shining too
    Then I'd take my darling Nelly Gray,
And we'd float down the river in my little red canoe,
    While my banjo sweetly I would play.

3

One night I went to see her but "she's gone!" the
    neighbors say,
    The white man bound her with his chain,
They have taken her to Georgia for to wear her life away,
    As she toils in the cotton and the cane.

4

My canoe is under water and my banjo is unstrung,
    I'm tired of living any more,
My eyes shall look downward and my songs shall be
    unsung
    While I stay on the old Kentucky shore.

5

My eyes are getting blinded and I cannot see my way,
    Hark! there's somebody knocking at the door—
Oh! I hear the angels calling and I see my Nelly Gray,
    Farewell to the old Kentucky shore.

CHORUS TO LAST VERSE

Oh! my darling Nelly Gray, up in heaven there they say,
    That they'll never take you from me any more,
I'm a coming—coming—coming, as the angels clear the
    way,
    Farewell to the old Kentucky shore.

1858

EDWARD HARRIGAN

(*David Braham, music*)

McNally's Row of Flats

It's down in Bottle Alley lives Timothy McNally,
A wealthy politician and a gentleman at that,
The joy of all the ladies, the gossoons and babies,
Who occupy the buildings call'd McNally's row of flats.

CHORUS
It's Ireland and Italy, Jerusalem and Germany,
Oh, Chinamen and nagers, and a paradise for cats,
All jumbled up togather in the snow or rainy weather,
They represent the tenants in McNally's row of flats.

2

The great conglomeration of men from ev'ry nation,
The Babylonian tower, oh! it could not equal that;
Peculiar institution, where brogues without dilution,
Were rattled off togcthcr in McNally's row of flats.

3

It's bags of rags and papers, with tramps and other sleepers,
Italian Lazaronees, there was lots of other rats,
A-lying on the benches, and dying then by inches
From open ventilation in McNally's row of flats.

It never was expected the rent would be collected,
They'd levy on the furniture, the bedding, and the slats!
You'd ought to see the rally and battle in the alley
A-throwing out the tenants from McNally's row of flats.

1882

No Wealth Without Labor

(*David Braham, music*)

The hand and the hammer are true loyal friends,
Between them no quarrels arise;
Oh, each on the other forever depends,
To gain labor's sweet golden prize.
The farmer, the blacksmith, and each working man,
While toiling for comfort and joy,
Remember the maxim, Oh, work all you can,
No wealth without labor, my boy.

CHORUS
Then cheer for the wage worker and toiler,
He's the builder of home and joys;
All riches must come after hard labor,
There's no wealth without it, boys.

2

The sea and the river unceasingly flow,
So grandly they both glide along;
Yes, all things in nature quite plainly do show
That God helps the weak and the strong.
The flower, the forest partake of the plan,

Of aiding our comfort and joy,
Remember the maxim, Oh, work all you can,
No wealth without labor, my boy.

3

The drone and the drunkard are helpless and sad
In Energy's joyous career,
Neglecting their chances they go to the bad,
And silently fall to the rear.
Ye steadfast and faithful, Oh, each sober man,
While turning for comfort and joy,
Remember the maxim, Oh, work all you can,
No wealth without labor, my boy.

1885

Samuel Woodworth's "The Hunters of Kentucky" (1824)

WAR SONGS

The Civil War could not have come at a worse time for Foster, creating a demand for different kinds of songs that his faltering talent could not satisfy. No wonder he sounded peeved in "That's What's the Matter":

> We live in hard and stirring times,
> Too sad for mirth, too rough for rhymes;
> For songs of peace have lost their chimes,
>   And that's what's the matter!

When he tried to rally 'round the flag or to tug at the heartstrings in "Was My Brother in the Battle?," Foster did so with less conviction and skill than George F. Root (1820–1895) and other songwriters who had begun their careers by emulating Foster.

Two of the most popular war songs during the peaceful decade of Foster's birth had been of necessity retrospective. "The Hunters of Kentucky," which commemorated Andrew Jackson's 1815 victory in the Battle of New Orleans, became the theme song of Old Hickory's presidential campaigns and anticipated the frontier bluster of "Jump Jim Crow" and "Old Dan Tucker" (as well as the history lesson in Johnny Horton's 1959 hit "The Battle of New Orleans," written by Jimmy Driftwood). Samuel Woodworth (1785–1842), the author of "The Hunters of Kentucky," also wrote the poem "The Bucket," which eventually became the nostalgic ballad (and implicit temperance song) "The Old Oaken Bucket."

In "The Minstrel's Returned from the War," John Hill Hewitt (1801–1890) looked back further than Woolworth and across the sea, to Sir Walter Scott's "The Lay of the Last Minstrel" and Tom Moore's "The Minstrel Boy." (The word "minstrel" had not yet become associated with blackface.) Although Hewitt once threatened to abandon songwriting "for the simple reason that it does not pay the author," he hung on to compose the music for two of the Civil War's most famous songs and win the sobriquet "the Bard of the Confederacy." Hewitt composed the most popular of many settings of Ethel Lynn Beer's poem "All Quiet Along the Potomac Tonight" and provided the music for "Somebody's Darling," poignant verses by Marie Ravenal de La Coste (1845–1936), a young resident of captive Savannah, Georgia.

It was Root, however, who profited the most from the Civil War. As a principal in the Chicago firm of Root & Cady, he published not only his own work, including the maudlin "Just Before the Battle, Mother" and the more hopeful "Tramp! Tramp! Tramp!," but also his setting of "The Vacant Chair," a poem by Henry Washburn (1813?–1903), and songs by Henry Clay Work, who was probably, after Root, the war's most successful Northern songwriter.

"Kingdom Coming" (see p. 39) was Work's first Civil War song; the triumphant "Marching Through Georgia" was his last. Published in 1865, it described with rose-colored retrospection the devastation wrought by General William Tecumseh Sherman. Issued the same year, "Tenting on the Old Camp Ground," by Walter Kittredge (1834–1905), took a more mournful and agonized view of the war that had yet to grind to a halt. The song was popularized by the Hutchinsons, fellow travelers in the campaigns for abolition and temperance with Kittredge, an itinerant singer and musician who also hailed from New Hampshire.

Ten years later, Harrigan and Braham's "The Regular Army O!" castigated, albeit comically, the injustice of coercing recently arrived immigrants to fight the nation's original Native American inhabitants.

STEPHEN C. FOSTER

That's What's the Matter

We live in hard and stirring times,
Too sad for mirth, too rough for rhymes;
For songs of peace have lost their chimes,
   And that's what's the matter!
The men we held as brothers true,
Have turn'd into a rebel crew;
So now we have to put them thro',
   And that's what's the matter!

CHORUS
That's what's the matter,
The rebels have to scatter;
We'll make them flee,
By land and sea,
And that's what's the matter!

2

Oh! yes, we thought our neighbors true,
Indulg'd them as their mothers do;
They storm'd our bright Red, White and Blue,
   And that's what's the matter!
We'll never give up what we gain,
For now we know we must maintain
Our Laws and Rights with might and main;
   And that's what's the matter!

3

The rebels thought we would divide,
And Democrats would take their side;
They then would let the Union slide,
   And that's what's the matter!
But, when the war had once begun,
All party feeling soon was gone;
We join'd as brothers, ev'ry one!
   And that's what's the matter!

4

The Merrimac, with heavy sway,
Had made our Fleet an easy prey—
The Monitor got in the way,
   And that's what's the matter!
So health to Captain Ericsson,
I cannot tell all he has done,
I'd never stop when once begun,
   And that's what's the matter!

5

We've heard of Gen'ral Beauregard,
And thought he'd fight us long and hard;
But he has play'd out his last card,
   And that's what's the matter!
So what's the use to fret and pout,
We soon will hear the people shout,
Secession dodge is *all* play'd out!
   And that's what's the matter!

1862

Was My Brother in the Battle?

Tell me, tell me weary soldier, from the rude and stirring
    wars,
Was my brother in the battle where you gained those
    noble scars?
He was ever brave and valiant, and I know he never fled,
Was his name among the wounded or numbered with
    the dead?
Was my brother in the battle when the tide of war ran
    high?
You would know him in a thousand by his dark and
    flashing eye.

CHORUS
Tell me, tell me weary soldier, will he never come again,
Did he suffer 'mid the wounded or die among the slain?

2

Was my brother in the battle when the noble Highland
    host
Were so wrongfully outnumbered on the Carolina coast;
Did he struggle for the Union 'mid the thunder and the
    rain,
Till he fell among the brave on a bleak Virginia plain?
Oh, I'm sure that he was dauntless and his courage ne'er
    would lag
While contending for the honor of our dear and
    cherished flag.

Was my brother in the battle when the flag of Erin came
To the rescue of our banner and protection of our fame,
While the fleet from off the waters poured out terror
    and dismay
Till the bold and erring foe fell like leaves on Autumn day?
When the bugle called to battle and the canon deeply
    roared,
Oh! I wish I could have seen him draw his sharp and
    glittering sword.

1862

SAMUEL WOODWORTH

New-Orleans (The Hunters of Kentucky)

Ye gentlemen and ladies fair,
    Who grace this famous city,
Just listen, if you've time to spare,
    While I rehearse a ditty;
And for the opportunity,
    Conceive yourselves quite lucky,
For 'tis not often that you see
    A hunter from Kentucky.

CHORUS
Oh, Kentucky—the hunters of Kentucky,
The hunters of Kentucky.

We are a hardy free-born race,
    Each man to fear a stranger,
Whate'er the game, we join in chase,
    Despising toil and danger.
And if a daring foe annoys,
    Whate'er his strength and forces,
We'll show him that Kentucky boys,
    Are alligator horses.

I s'pose you've read it in the prints,
    How Packenham attempted
To make Old Hickory Jackson wince,
    But soon his scheme repented.
For we, with rifles ready cock'd,
    Thought such occasion lucky,
And soon around the general flock'd
    The hunters of Kentucky.

You've heard, I s'pose, how New-Orleans
    Is fam'd for wealth and beauty—
There's girls of every hue, it seems,
    From snowy white to sooty.
So Packenham, he made his brags,
    If he in fight was lucky,
He'd have their girls and cotton bags,
    In spite of old Kentucky.

But Jackson, he was wide awake,
    And wasn't scared at trifles;
For well he knew what aim we take,
    With our Kentucky rifles.

So he led us down to Cypress swamp,
  The ground was low and mucky;
There stood John Bull in martial pomp,
  And *here* was old Kentucky.

A bank was raised to hide our breast,
  Not that we thought of dying,
But then we always like to rest,
  Unless the game is flying.
Behind it stood our little force,
  None wish'd it to be greater,
For every man was half a horse,
  And half an alligator.

They did not let our patience tire
  Before they show'd their faces,
We did not choose to waste our fire,
  So snugly kept our places.
But when so near we see them wink,
  We thought it time to stop 'em,
And 'twould have done you good, I think,
  To see Kentuckians drop 'em.

They found, at last, 'twas vain to fight,
  Where *lead* was all their *booty*;
And so they wisely took to flight,
  And left *us* all the *beauty*.
And now if danger e'er annoys,
  Remember what our trade is,
Just send for us Kentucky boys,
  And we'll protect ye, ladies.

1821

JOHN HILL HEWITT

The Minstrel's Return from the War

The minstrel's return'd from the war,
With spirits as buoyant as air;
And thus on his tuneful guitar,
He sings in the bow'r of his fair;
The noise of battle is o'er,
The bugle no more calls to arms;
A soldier no more but a lover,
I kneel to the pow'r of thy charms!
   Sweet Lady, dear Lady! I'm thine,
   I bend to the magic of beauty;
   Tho' the helmit and banner are mine,
   Yet love calls the soldier to duty.

2

The minstrel his suit warmly prest,
She blush'd, sigh'd, and hung down her head;
'Till conquer'd she fell on his breast,
And thus to the happy youth said:
"The bugle shall part us, love, never,
My bosom thy pillow shall be;
'Till death tears thee from me for ever
Still faithful I'll perish with thee!"
   Sweet Lady, dear Lady! I'm thine,
   I bend to the magic of beauty;
   Tho' the helmit and banner are mine,
   Yet love calls the soldier to duty.

But fame called the youth to the field,
His banner wav'd over his head;
He gave his guitar for a shield,
But soon he laid low with the dead:
While she o'er her young hero bending,
Received his expiring adieu;
"I die while my country defending,
With heart to my lady love true."
  "Oh! death!" then she sigh'd, "I am thine,
  I tear off the roses of beauty,
  For the grave of my hero is mine,
  He died true to love and to duty."

1838; written 1825

HENRY S. WASHBURN

(*George F. Root, music*)

The Vacant Chair

(*Thanksgiving, 1861*)

We shall meet, but we shall miss him
There will be one vacant chair;
We shall linger to caress him
While we breathe our evening prayer.
When a year ago we gathered,
Joy was in his mild blue eye,
But a golden cord is severed,
And our hopes in ruin lie.

We shall meet, but we shall miss him,
There will be one vacant chair;
We shall linger to caress him
When we breathe our evening prayer.

2

At our fireside, sad and lonely,
Often will the bosom swell
At remembrance of the story
How our noble Willie fell;
How he strove to bear our banner
Thro' the thickest of the fight,
And uphold our country's honor,
In strength of manhood's might.

3

True they tell us wreaths of glory
Ever more will deck his brow,
But this soothes the anguish only
Sweeping o'er our heartstrings now.
Sleep today, O early fallen,
In thy green and narrow bed,
Dirges from the pine and cypress
Mingle with the tears we shed.

1861

GEORGE F. ROOT

Just Before the Battle, Mother

Just before the battle, Mother,
I am thinking most of you;
While upon the field we're watching,
With the enemy in view.
Comrades brave are round me lying,
Fill'd with tho'ts of home and God;
For well they know, that on the morrow,
Some will sleep beneath the sod.

CHORUS
Farewell Mother, you may never
Press me to your heart again;
But O, you'll not forget me, Mother,
If I'm number'd with the slain.

2

Oh, I long to see you, Mother;
And the loving ones at home;
But, I'll never leave our banner,
Till in honor I can come.
Tell the traitors, all around you,
That their cruel words, we know,
In ev'ry battle kill our soldiers
By the help they give the foe.

Hark! I hear the bugles sounding,
Tis the signal for the fight,
Now may God protect us, Mother,
As He ever does the right.
Hear the "Battle-Cry of Freedom,"*
How it swells upon the air;
Oh, yes we'll rally round the standard,
Or we'll perish nobly there.

1862

*In the Army of the Cumberland, the Soldiers sing the Battle-Cry when going into action, by order of the Commanding General.

Tramp! Tramp! Tramp!
(The Prisoner's Hope)

In the prison cell I sit,
Thinking Mother dear, of you,
And our bright and happy home so far away,
And the tears they fill my eyes
Spite of all that I can do,
Tho' I try to cheer my comrades and be gay.

CHORUS
Tramp, tramp, tramp, the boys are marching,
Cheer up comrades they will come,
And beneath the starry flag
We shall breathe the air again,
Of the freeland in our own beloved home.

2

In the battle front we stood
When their fiercest charge they made,
And they swept us off a hundred men or more,
But before we reach'd their lines
They were beaten back dismayed,
And we heard the cry of vict'ry o'er and o'er.

3

So within the prison cell,
We are waiting for the day
That shall come to open wide the iron door,
And the hollow eye grows bright,
And the poor heart almost gay,
As we think of seeing home and friends once more.

1862

MARIE RAVENAL DE LA COSTE

(*John Hill Hewitt, music*)

Somebody's Darling

Into the ward of the clean whitewash'd halls,
    Where the dead slept and the dying lay;
Wounded by bayonets, sabres and balls,
    Somebody's darling was borne one day.
Somebody's darling, so young and so brave,
    Wearing still on his sweet yet pale face,—
Soon to be hid in the dust of the grave,
    The lingering light of his boyhood's grace.

Somebody's darling—Somebody's pride—
Who'll tell his mother where her boy died.

2

Matted and damp are his tresses of gold,
    Kissing the snow of that fair young brow;
Pale are the lips of most delicate mould,
    Somebody's darling is dying now.
Back from his beautiful purple-vein'd brow,
    Brush off the wand'ring waves of gold;
Cross his white hands on his broad bosom now.
    Somebody's darling is still and cold.

3

Give him a kiss, but for Somebody's sake,
    Murmur a prayer for him, soft and low;
One little curl from his golden mates take,
    Somebody's pride they were once, you know;
Somebody's warm hand has oft rested there,
    Was it a mother's, so soft and white?
Or have the lips of a sister, so fair,
    Ever been bath'd in their waves of light?

4

Somebody's watching and waiting for him,
    Yearning to hold him again to her breast;
Yet there he lies with his blue eyes so dim,
    And purple, child-like lips half apart.

Tenderly bury the fair unknown dead,
    Pausing to drop on his grave a tear;
Carve on the wooden slab over his head,
    Somebody's darling is slumbering here.

1864

WALTER KITTREDGE

Tenting on the Old Camp Ground

We're tenting tonight on the old Camp ground,
Give us a song to cheer
Our weary hearts, a song of home,
And friends we love so dear.

CHORUS
Many are the hearts that are weary tonight,
Wishing for the war to cease;
Many are the hearts looking for the right
To see the dawn of peace.
Tenting to night, Tenting to night,
Tenting on the old Camp ground.

2

We've been tenting tonight on the old Camp ground,
Thinking of days gone by,
Of the lov'd ones at home that gave us the hand,
And the tear that said, "Good bye!"

We are tired of war on the old Camp ground,
Many are dead and gone,
Of the brave and true who've left their homes,
Others been wounded long.

We've been fighting today on the old Camp ground,
Many are lying near;
Some are dead and some are dying,
Many are in tears.

CHORUS (LAST VERSE)
Many are the hearts that are weary tonight,
Wishing for the war to cease;
Many are the hearts looking for the right
To see the dawn of peace.
Dying tonight, Dying tonight,
Dying on the old Camp ground.

1864

HENRY CLAY WORK

Marching Through Georgia

Bring the good old bugle, boys! we'll sing another song—
Sing it with a spirit that will start the world along—
Sing it as we used to sing it, fifty thousand strong,
While we were marching through Georgia.

"Hurrah! Hurrah! we bring the Jubilee!
Hurrah! Hurrah! the flag that makes you free!"
So we sang the chorus from Atlanta to the sea,
While we were marching through Georgia.

2

How the darkeys shouted when they heard the joyful
    sound!
How the turkeys gobbled which our commissary found!
How the sweet potatoes even started from the ground,
While we were marching through Georgia.

3

Yes, and there were Union men who wept with joyful
    tears,
When they saw the honor'd flag they had not seen for
    years;
Hardly could they be restrained from breaking forth in
    cheers,
While we were marching through Georgia.

4

"Sherman's dashing Yankee boys will never reach the
    coast!"
So the saucy rebels said, and 'twas a handsome boast,
Had they not forgot, alas! to reckon with the host,
While we were marching through Georgia.

So we made a thoroughfare for Freedom and her train,
Sixty miles in latitude—three hundred to the main;
Treason fled before us, for resistance was in vain,
While we were marching through Georgia.

1865

EDWARD HARRIGAN

(*David Braham, music*)

The Regular Army O!

Three years ago, this very day,
We went to Governor's Isle;
For to stand forninst the cannon,
In true military style.
Seventeen American dollars,
Each month we surely get,
For to carry a gun, and bagnetts
With a regimental step.
We had our choice of going
To the army, or to jail;
Or it's up the Hudson river,
With a "copper" take a sail:
Oh we puckered up our courage,
Wid bravery we did go,
Oh we cursed the day we went away
Wid the Regular Army O!

There was Sergeant John McCaffery,
And Captain Donahue,
Oh they make us march, and toe the mark,
In gallant Company "Q,"
Oh, the drums would roll upon my soul,
This is the style we'd go
Forty miles a day, on beans and hay,
In the Regular Army O!

2

We wint to Arizony
For to fight the Injins there;
We came near being made bald-headed,
But they never got our hair;
We lay among the ditches,
In the yellow dirty mud,
And we never saw an onion,
A turnip, or a spud.
Oh we were taken prisoners,
Conveyed forninst the Chafe,
Oh he said we'll make an Irish stew,
The dirty Indian thafe.
On the telegraphic wire
We walked to Mexico
We bless the day we skipped away
From the Regular Army O!

3

We've been dry as army herrings,
And as hungry as a Turk;
Oh the boys along the street cry out,

"Soger, would you work?"
We'd ship into the Navy
For to plow the raging sea,
But cold water sure we couldn't endure,
'Twould never agree wid me.
We'll join the politicians,
Then we know we'll be well fed,
Oh we'll sleep no more upon the ground,
But in a feather bed.
And if a war it should break out,
They call on us to go.
We'll git Italian substitutes
For the Regular Army O!

    4

We've corns upon our heels, my boys,
And bunions on our toes:
From lugging a gun in the red hot sun,
Puts freckles on our nose.
England has its Grenadiers,
France has its Zoo-zoos,
The U.S.A. never changes they say:
But continually wear the blues.
When we are out upon parade
We must have our muskets bright,
Or they'll slap us in the guard-house,
To pass away the night.
And whin we want a furlough,
To the Colonel we do go;
He says—go to bed, and wait till you're dead,
In the Regular Army O!

1874

Edward Harrigan (c. 1880)

COMIC SONGS

The most memorable and distinctive lyrics that George Cooper furnished during Foster's declining years were comic. Many of Foster's plantation melodies had been humorous, but these songs were different. In addition to eschewing blackface dialect, they were wordier, more theatrical, and their patter proceeded at a faster pace. Instead of harking back to minstrel shows, they looked ahead to the developing venue of vaudeville, which presented a variety of acts that included but were by no means limited to minstrels and which sought to please a broader, more genteel audience. Even a husband's drunken hiccup does not seriously disrupt the respectable domesticity of "My Wife Is a Most Knowing Woman" or "Mr. and Mrs. Brown."

The differences between Henry S. Thompson's 1863 "Down by the River Lived a Maiden," the earliest known version of "Oh My Darling Clementine," and Percy Montrose's more familiar 1884 rendition illustrate the shift. Thompson's blackface dialect (however inconsistent) and grotesque depiction of the ill-featured and -fated Clementine were in the bawdy tradition of minstrelsy. Montrose preserved some of the song's jokes but whitewashed the language, switched the scene to the California Gold Rush, and omitted that Clementine had fallen into the drink because she was drunk. (Thompson, incidentally, seems to have been born in 1824 or 1825, but the date of his death is unknown. Montrose is a cipher. Popular songwriters in the latter half of the 19th century have been the subject of so little research that in many instances their dates of birth and death must be left blank. The identity of "Blasee," for example, who penned the lyrics to "The Girl That Keeps the Peanut Stand," remains a mystery.)

The unsavory origin of "Oh Where, Oh Where Is My Little Dog Gone" is to be found in "Der Deitcher's Dog," by Septimus Winner (1827–1902), which is also a reminder that the accents of German immigrants could provoke as much derision as an Irish brogue or African-American argot. Vaudeville's foremost impresario, Tony Pastor, was Italian, born Antonio, yet Irish-American songwriters predominated in the latter half of the 19th century as incontrovertibly as Jewish songwriters would in the first half of the 20th. Although their indulgence in dialect and ethnic stereotypes can sound to our ears almost as demeaning as blackface, unlike minstrelsy's predominantly white composers they were writing about their own kind instead of the Other, and they did so with fond knowledge. While the prolific Edward Harrigan was a marvel of consistency, many another writer, such as Joseph Flynn, half of the vaudeville duo of Sheridan and Flynn, composed one uproarious hit (in Flynn's case, "Down Went McGinty") and returned to obscurity. Another vaudevillian, Joe Hart (1861–1921), brings this anthology full circle by celebrating in "Globe Trotting Nellie Bly" an intrepid reporter who began her career in Pittsburgh and borrowed her byline from Stephen Foster's "Nelly Bly."

GEORGE COOPER

(*Stephen Foster, music*)

My Wife Is a Most Knowing Woman

My wife is a most knowing woman,
    She always is finding me out,
She never will hear explanations
    But instantly puts me to rout,
There's no use to try to deceive her,
    If out with my friends, night or day,
In the most inconceivable manner
    She tells where I've been right away,
She says that I'm "mean" and "inhuman"
    Oh! my wife is a most knowing woman.

2

She would have been hung up for witchcraft
    If she had lived sooner, I know,
There's no hiding any thing from her,
    She knows what I do—where I go;
And if I come in after midnight
    And say "I have been to the lodge,"
Oh, she says while she flies into a fury,
    "Now don't think to play such a dodge!
It's all very fine, but won't do, man,"
    Oh, my wife is a most knowing woman.

3

Not often I go out to dinner
    And come home a little "so so,"
I try to creep up through the hall-way,
    As still as a mouse, on tip-toe,
She's sure to be waiting up for me
    And then comes a nice little scene,
"What, you tell me you're sober, you wretch you,
    Now don't think I am so green!
My life is quite worn out with you, man,"
    Oh, my wife is a most knowing woman!

4

She knows *me* much better than *I do*,
    Her eyes are like those of a lynx,
Though how she discovers my secrets
    Is a riddle would puzzle a sphynx,
On fair days, when we go out walking,
    If ladies look at me askance,
In the most harmless way, I assure you,
    My wife gives me, oh! such a glance,
And says "all these insults you'll rue, man,"
    Oh, my wife is a most knowing woman.

5

Yes, I must give all of my friends up
    If I would live happy and quiet;
One might as well be 'neath a tombstone
    As live in confusion and riot.
This life we all know is a short one,
    While *some* tongues are long, heaven knows,

And a miserable life is a husbands,
    Who numbers his wife with his foes,
I'll stay at home now like a true man,
    For my wife is a most knowing woman.

                                                        1863

If You've Only Got a Moustache

Oh! all of you poor single men,
    Don't ever give up in despair,
For there's always a chance while there's life
    To capture the hearts of the fair,
No matter what may be your age,
    You always may cut a fine dash,
You will suit all the girls to a hair
    If you've only got a moustache,
        A moustache, a moustache
        If you've only got a moustache.

        2
No matter for manners or style,
    No matter for birth or for fame,
All these *used* to have something to do
    With young ladies changing their name,
There's no reason now to despond,
    Or go and do any thing rash,
For you'll do though you can't raise a cent,
    If you'll only raise a moustache!
        A moustache, a moustache,
        If you'll only raise a moustache.

3

Your head may be thick as a block,
    And empty as any foot-ball,
Oh! your eyes may be green as the grass
    Your heart just as hard as a wall.
Yet take the advice that I give,
    You'll soon gain affection and cash,
And will be all the rage with the girls,
    If you'll only get a moustache,
        A moustache, a moustache,
        If you'll only get a moustache.

4

I once was in sorrow and tears
    Because I was jilted you know,
So right down to the river I ran
    To quickly dispose of my woe,
A good friend he gave me advice
    And timely prevented the splash,
Now at home I've a wife and ten heirs,
    And all through a handsome moustache,
        A moustache, a moustache,
        And all through a handsome moustache.

1864

Mr. & Mrs. Brown

MRS. BROWN:	So Mister Brown you've come at last,
	I'm sure it's after two.
MR. BROWN:	Dear Mistress Brown, your clock is fast,
	I know as well as you.
MRS. BROWN:	Oh! Sir, it's shameful so it is,
	Don't come sir in my sight!
MR. BROWN:	Now give me one good kiss to night,
	You see that I'm all right.
MRS. BROWN:	I cannot talk to you to night,
	I see that you're not right.
	Oh! Harry Brown! O! Harry Brown!
	You're anything but right.
MR. BROWN:	Now give me one good kiss to night,
	You see that I'm all right.
	Oh! Mary Brown! O! Mary Brown!
	You know that I'm all right.

2

SHE:	All right! you good for nothing you,
	Have I not eyes to see?
HE:	No Madam, what I say is true,
	I'm only on a spree!
SHE:	Don't make me angry, Mr. Brown,
	For if you do I'll cry!
HE:	I shall not stay to see you frown,
	So, Mrs. Brown, good bye.
HE:	I shall not stay to see you frown,
BOTH:	So, Mrs. Brown, good bye.
SHE:	I'll make you stay to see me frown,
	You shall not say good bye.

He:	O! Mary Brown, O! Mary Brown,
Both:	I'll have to say good bye.
She:	O! Harry Brown, O! Harry Brown,
	You see you've made me cry.

3

She (*Furiously*):

Hard hearted man, I tell you what,
  I must know where you've been;
I am not jealous, O! no! no!
  But it's a shame and sin!
Your bosom friend, young Jones, just left,
  He calls here every night,
I'm sure if it were not for him
  I'd really die with fright.

She:	I'm sure if it were not for him,
Both:	I'd really die with fright.
He:	What Ma'am, if it were not for him
	You say you'd die with fright!
He:	O! Mary Brown, O! Mary Brown,
Both:	I'll call him out to fight!
She:	O! Harry Brown, O! Harry Brown,
	He's far above your height.

4

He (*Indignantly*):

So, Mr. Jones was here, you say
  While I have been away!
Now Madam you will drive me mad,
  We part this very day.
You know it is my business ma'am
  That keeps me at the store,

And if I could have sooner come (*hic*)
I'd been here (*hic*) long before.

HE: You know it is my business ma'am

BOTH: That keeps me at the store.

SHE: I know it's not your business, sir
That keeps you at the store.

HE: O! Mary Brown, O! Mary Brown,

BOTH: It's business at the store.

SHE: O! Harry Brown, O! Harry Brown,
You've told me that before.

5

SHE (*Coaxingly*):

There, don't be angry, husband, don't!
I'm sure I love you dear,
I was but joking when I said
That odious Jones was here.
But promise me, now wont you love,
That when the night has come
You'll never stay away so late,
And leave your wife at home.

SHE: Now promise me when night has come,

BOTH: You'll always stay at home.

HE: I'll promise you when night has come
I'll always stay at home.

HE: O! Mary Brown, O! Mary Brown,

BOTH: I'll always stay at home.

SHE: O! Harry Brown, O! Harry Brown,
Now won't you stay at home?

6

HE (*Lovingly*):

You were but joking, dearest wife?
  Now come and kiss me, do,
Jones is a bosom friend to me, (*seriously*)
  But needn't be to you.
My little wife! my joy and life!
  My gentle pretty elf,
If any one sits up with you
  Hereafter, it's myself.

HE: If any one sits up with you
BOTH: Hereafter, it's myself.
SHE: If any one sits up with me,
              O, let it be yourself.

HE: O! Mary Brown, O! Mary Brown,
BOTH: Our quarrels they are o'er.
SHE: O! Harry Brown, O! Harry Brown,
              We'll never quarrel more.

1864

WILLIAM STARK

(*The Hutchinson Family Singers, music*)

The Modern Belle

The daughter sits in the parlor,
    And rocks in the easy chair—
She is dressed in her silks and satins,
    And jewels are in her hair.
She smiles and she sniggles and simpers,
    And simpers and sniggles and winks;
And although she talks but a little,
    'Tis vastly more than she thinks.

2

Her father goes clad in his russets,
    And ragged and seedy at that;
His coat is out at the elbows,
    And he wears a most shocking bad hat.
He is hoarding and saving his shillings,
    So carefully day by day,
While she with her beaus and poodles,
    Is throwing them all away.

3

She lies abed in the morning
    Till almost the hour of noon,
And comes down snapping and snarling
    Because they have called her so soon.
Her hair is still in the papers,

Her cheeks still daubed with paint—
Remains of her last night's blushes,
  Before she intended to faint.

   4

Her feet are so very little,
  Her hands are so very white!
Her jewels are so very heavy,
  And her head so very light!
Her color is made of cosmetics,
  But this she will never own;
Her body's made mostly of cotton,
  Her heart is made wholly of stone.

   5

She falls in love with a fellow
  Who swells with a foreign air;
He marries her for her money,
  She marries him for his hair.
One of the very best matches!
  Both are well mated in life;
She's got a fool for a husband,
  And he's got a fool for a wife.

1851

H. S. THOMPSON

Down by the River Lived a Maiden

Down by the river there lived a maiden,
In a cottage built just seven by nine,
And all around this lubly bower,
The beauteous sunflower blossoms twine.

CHORUS
Oh! my Clema, Oh! my Clema,
Oh! my darling Clementine,
Now you are gone and lost forever,
I'm drefful sorry Clementine.

2

Her lips were like two luscious beefsteaks
Dipp'd in tomato sass and brine,
And like the cashmere goatess covering
Was the fine wool of Clementine.

3

Her foot, Oh! Golly! Twas a beauty,
Her shoes were made of Digby pine,
Two herring boxes without the tops on
Just made the sandals of Clementine.

4

One day de wind was blowing awful
I took her down some old rye wine,
And listened to de sweetest cooings,
Ob my sweet sunflower Clementine.

5

De ducks had gone down to de riber,
To drive dem back she did incline,
She stubb'd her toe and Oh! Kersliver,
She fell into the foamy brine.

6

I see'd her lips above de waters,
A blowing bubbles bery fine,
But 'twant no use I want no swimmer,
And so I lost my Clementine.

7

Now ebry night down by de riber,
Her ghostess walks bout half past nine
I know tis her a kase I tracked her,
And by de smell tis Clementine.

8

Now all young men by me take warning,
Don't gib your ladies too much rye wine,
Kase like as not in this wet wedder,
Dey'll share de fate ob Clementine.

1863

PERCY MONTROSE

Oh My Darling Clementine

In a cabin, in a canon,
An excavation for a mine;
Dwelt a miner, a Forty-niner,
And his daughter Clementine

CHORUS
Oh my darling, Oh my darling,
Oh my darling Clementine,
You are lost and gone forever,
Drefful sorry, Clementine.

2

She drove her ducklets, to the river,
Ev'ry morning just at nine;
She stubb'd her toe, against a sliver,
And fell into the foaming brine.

3

I saw her lips above the water,
Blowing bubbles soft and fine;
Alas for me, I was no swimmer,
And so I lost my Clementine.

1884

SEPTIMUS WINNER

Der Deitcher's Dog

Oh where, Oh where ish mine little dog gone;
Oh where, Oh where can he be . . .
His ears cut short und his tail cut long:
Oh where, Oh where ish he.

CHORUS
Tra la la la la la la la la la la,
la la la la la la la la la la,
Tra la la la la la la la la la la,
la la la la la la . . .

2

I loves mine lager 'tish very goot beer,
Oh where, Oh where can he be . . .
But mit no money I cannot drink here.
Oh where, Oh where ish he . . .

3

Across the ocean in Garmanie,
Oh where, Oh where can he be . . .
Der deitchers dog ish der best companie.
Oh where, Oh where ish he . . .

4

Un sasage ish goot, bolonie of course,
Oh, where, Oh where can he be . . .
Dey makes um mit dog und dey makes em mit horse,
I guess de makes em mit he . . .

1864

"BLASEE"

(*Albert Harry, music*)

The Girl That Keeps the Peanut Stand

I wander'd down the other day,
    Along the river strand,
And there I met the pretty maid
    That keeps the peanut stand
I ogled her, she ogled me,
    She looked so very grand
None can surpass the blooming lass
    That keeps the peanut stand.

CHORUS

Oh! (*Spoken:* "You just ought to have seen her.")
She dress'd so neat, she look'd so sweet
I couldn't hardly stand,
My heart it palpitated so, it shook the peanut stand.

2

Her hair was frizzled o'er her brow,
    Her eyes were slightly cross'd,
Her face was thickly freckled o'er
    Like mildew mix'd with frost,
Her gown of richest calico
    Hung low upon her neck,
And sundry graces round her shed,
    With spots of grease bedeck'd.

3

I mosied up, "how do you do,
    My pretty lass I pray"
"I'm hunkadora how are you,
    Come buy some nuts to day."
Said I "I'll take a half a pint
    If you will sell 'em low,
And throw me in a kiss to boot,"
    Said she, "go long old blow"

4

I asked her if she'd like to have
    A man of my estate,
She monched a handfull of peanuts,
    And said, "you've come too late,
I am the organ grinder's girl
    And him I mean to wed.
Do you suppose I'd give him up
    And marry you instead?"

5

Oh ! how I love that peanut girl,
    No one can ever know,
I wish that organ grinder man
    Was grinding down below;
And now a broken hearted man,
    I wander through the land,
My soul a busten for the gal
    What keeps the peanut stand.

If I could play the organ well
   I'd go to grinding too,
And I would cut as big a swell
   As other grinders do;
But as I didn't go to war,
   And lose a leg or hand,
I've lost for aye my pretty lass
   That keeps the peanut stand.

1868

EDWARD HARRIGAN

(*David Braham, music*)

Sweet Mary Ann

My Mary Ann's a teacher in a great big public school,
She gets one thousand dollars every year.
She has charge of all the children—you'd never find a
     fool,
For Mary gives them all the proper steer.
For she studied Greek and Latin, real French and
     Timbuctoo,
Yes German Spanish Turk and Hindostan.
Sweet Portuguese and Irish and Jerusalam Hebrew—
Such an Education has my Mary Ann.

She's a darling, she's a daisy,
She's a dumpling, she's a lamb.
You should hear her play on the piana—
Such an Education has my Mary Ann.

2

My Mary Ann's a lady, no contemptible coquette,
When I meet her sure my heart goes in a dream.
She's thoroughly conversant with the art of etiquette,
And at cards she'd beat old Hoyle himself a game.
Oh she'd play you Whist or Cribbage, Forty-fives or
    Casino,
And she'd deal the cards just like a Gambler man.
At Poker or Peaknucle or Saky or Pedro—
Such an Education has my Mary Ann.

3

My Mary Ann's a dancer in the art of terpsichore,
You should see her forward four an alamande.
She'd break up all the lumber that you'd lay down on
    the floor,
Such a heavy stepper is my Mary Ann.
Oh she'd dance you the Mazurka, a Polka or Quadrille,
A Reel and Jig or shuffle in the sand.
The Schottisch or the German you could not keep her
    still—
Such an Education has my Mary Ann.

                                                    1878

Down in Gossip Row

(*David Braham, music*)

I moved my fam'ly bed and all last year the first of May,
From a very quiet neighborhood, sure, Dan coaxed me
    away,
Hypocrisy and scandal, they have caused me bitter woe,
Oh ever since the morning, I moved down in Gossip Row.

CHORUS
Good morning Misses Dooley, and did you hear the news,
Sure, Mary Quinn went to a ball, and borrow'd Katy's
    shoes,
There's a second-hand piano in twenty-two below,
And lots of drunken boarders in that house in Gossip Row.
Now, listen Misses Crowley, I've something for your ear.
What is it dear? what is it? oh, we're dying for to hear.
The brunette, Julia Dempsey, I'm told she has a beau,
She run off wid a soger from her house in Gossip Row.

2

I wear a new-made bonnet oh, and walk along the block,
How they poke their heads from windows and they
    whisper what a shock,
She thinks she is a young schoolgirl, ain't she a horrid
    show,
Ye'd have to run the gauntlet, when ye walk in Gossip
    Row.

Good evening Misses Dooley, oh, did you have your tea,
I had a glass of lager beer, just now with Missis Fay,
She wants to be a Yankee, I'll let the neighbors know,
She lived in County Connaught for she moved in Gossip
    Row.
Now, listen Misses Crowley, I never like to speak,
But who throws out the garbage ev'ry Sunday in the week,
Sure, I could tell ye aisy, go on, we want to know,
'Tis Misses Lynch, ah, ha, ha, ha, that lives in Gossip Row.

3

They borrow'd all my kindling wood and dove into my
    coal,
Sure, they walk'd off with my crockery 'cept one old
    sugar bowl,
My overcoat and tab jacket, I need it for the snow,
Were stole off from the clothesline, in my yard in
    Gossip Row.

CHORUS

Oh, dear me Misses Dooley, I went to Coney Isle,
The old man was not home 'till six, you flirted there a
    while,
I met a German bugler, yes, yes, we want to know,
He eat clams with the lady that is known in Gossip Row.
Excuse me, Misses Crowley, now won't you take a chair,
I'm told that Misses Coogan she is dying up her hair,
Her little daughter, Delia, she's sent off to Bordo,
To learn the polly woo, woo, for the French in Gossip
    Row.

1880

Cash! Cash! Cash!

(*David Braham, music*)

At Macy's grand Emporium
I met a charmer fair,
Oh, she was selling neckties
To the swells that gather'd there;
I stepped up to the counter,
I said my name is Frash,
Said I, my pretty little girl,
She simply hollow'd cash!

CHORUS
It was cash! cash! cash!
With a smash, smash, smash,
Oh, she hammer'd on the counter
For number forty-nine;
It was cash! cash! cash!
I thought I had a mash,
But when I went to speak to her,
'Twas cash! cash! cash!

2

I asked her for a price-list, then
She handed me a book,
Oh, then I looked it over
For to see if she would look,
She never condescended,
Which made me rather brash,
Said I, my pretty little girl,
She simply murmur'd cash!

3

I paid her for a necktie,
A regular bonton,
I asked if she'd be so kind
To help me put it on,
She leaned across the counter
In a manner very rash,
I kiss'd her on her pretty cheek
She simply hollow'd cash!

4

Up came a little pretty child
About the age of nine,
She whisper'd softly to him:
"Call hither Mister Ryan,"
A monster large Hibernian,
He hit me such a smash;
As I went out through the doorway,
Oh, I heard her hollow cash!

1881

BILLY MORTIMER

(*Dan Lewis, music*)

Fifty Cents

I took my girl to a fancy ball,
It was a social hop.
We staid until the folks went out
And the music it did stop.
Then to a restaurant we went
The best one on the street.
She said she was not hungry,
But this is what she eat.
A dozen raw, a plate of slaw,
A chicken and a roast,
Some sparrow grass with apple sass,
And soft shell crabbs on toast.
A big box stew with crackers, too;
Her hunger was immense.
When She called for pie,
I thought I'd die, for I had but fifty cents . . .

2

She said so sweet that she was not well,
And she did not care to eat
Now I have money in my clothes
That says she can't be beat.
I asked her what she'd have to drink,
She's got an awful tank.
She said she was not thirsty

But this is what she drank.
A glass of jin, a whiskey skin,
It made me shake with fear.
Some ginger pop, with rum on top,
A schooner, then, of beer.
A glass of ale, a gin cocktail,
She ought to have had more sense.
When She called for more
I dropped on the floor
For I had but fifty cents . . .

3

I told her that my head did ache,
And I did not care to eat
Expecting every moment
To get kicked into the street.
She said she'd bring her fam'ly round,
Some day and have some fun.
I gave the clerk the fifty cents
And this is what he done.
He smashed my nose and tore my clothes
And hit me in the jaw.
He put my eyes in mourning deep
And with me swept the floor;
He grabbed me where my pants were loose
And kicked me o'er the fence.
Take my advice don't try it twice
When you have but fifty cents . . .

1881

Down Went McGinty

Sunday morning just at nine,
Dan McGinty dress'd so fine,
Stood looking up at a very high stone wall;
When his friend young Pat McCann,
Says, I'll bet you five dollars, Dan,
I could carry you to the top without a fall;
So on his shoulders he took Dan,
To climb the ladder he began,
And soon he commenc'd to reach up near the top;
When McGinty, cute old rogue,
To win the five he did let go,
Never thinking just how far he'd have to drop.

CHORUS
Down went McGinty to the bottom of the wall,
And tho' he won five,
He more dead than alive,
Sure his ribs, and nose, and back were broke from getting
such a fall,
Dress'd in his best suit of clothes.

2

From the hospitle Mac went home,
When they fix'd his broken bones,
To find he was the father of a child;
So to celebrate it right,
His friends he went to invite,

And he soon was drinking whisky fast and wild;
    Then he waddled down the street
    In his Sunday suit so neat,
Holding up his head as proud as John the Great,
    But in the sidewalk was a hole,
    To receive a ton of coal,
That McGinty never saw till just too late.

CHORUS

Down went McGinty to the bottom of the hole,
    Then the driver of the cart
    Give the load of coal a start,
And it took us half an hour to dig McGinty from the coal,
    Dress'd in his best suit of clothes.

3

Now McGinty raved and swore,
About his clothes he felt so sore,
And an oath he took he'd kill the man or die;
    So he tightly grabb'd his stick
    And hit the driver a lick,
Then he raised a little shanty on his eye;
    But two policemen saw the muss
    And they soon join'd in the fuss,
Then they ran McGinty in for being drunk;
    And the Judge says with a smile,
    We will keep you for a while
In a cell to sleep upon a prison bunk.

Down went McGinty to the bottom of the jail
   Where his board would cost him nix,
   And he stay'd exactly six,
They were big long months he stopp'd
   For no one went his bail,
   Dress'd in his best suit of clothes.

   4

   Now McGinty thin and pale
   One fine day got out of jail,
And with joy to see his boy was nearly wild;
   To his house he quickly ran
   To meet his wife Bedaley Ann,
But she'd skipp'd away and took along the child;
   Then he gave up in despair,
   And he madly pull'd his hair,
As he stood one day upon the river shore,
   Knowing well he couldn't swim,
   He did foolishly jump in,
Although water he had never took before.

CHORUS

Down went McGinty to the bottom of the bay,
   And he must be very wet
   For they haven't found him yet,
But they say his ghost comes round the docks
   Before the break of day,
   Dress'd in his best suit of clothes

1889

JOE HART

Globe Trotting Nellie Bly

I hold here in my hand a lengthy cablegram,
    That came from far across the sea;
It's from Miss Nellie Bly,
    And its contents I will try
To tell, if you listen unto me.
    She's trying very hard
To beat the world's record
    To round the world in seventy-five days;
Of the many funny sights in her Cablegram she writes,
    Of the people and their very curious ways.

CHORUS
With an umbrella and a grip,
    She gave her friends the slip,
Far across the deep blue sea;
    It was a pleasant trip,
For her grip was not "La Grippe,"
    Consequently she was as happy as could be.

2

When she landed in Cork, to Killarney took a walk,
    And kissed the blarney stone with her sweet lips;
She told funny tales to the Prince of Wales,
    And left him laughing almost in a fit.
She did the Gaiety dance and set Paris in a trance,
    Sang "Little Annie Rooney" to Jules Verne;

She would have spoken French and Greek, if she could
    have stayed a week,
  But she knew fond hearts for her at home did yearn.

CHORUS
She cheered up all the crew
  With a little song or two,
At sea she ate three times a day,
  From the bottom of the sea,
Up came McGinty,
  To wish her luck upon her way.

3

When she landed in Hong Kong, she rang the dinner
    gong,
  And they thought her quite a curiosity.
To see our Nelly hustle, and she did not wear a bustle,
  A sight which even here we rarely see.
When she reached Yokohama she met a Jersey farmer,
  And together they sipped too-long boo-long tea;
She was courted by a Jap—sat in the old King's lap,
  And he wanted her to marry him, you see.

CHORUS
But when the Oceanic sailed,
  How that poor fellow wailed,
Now she's on the ocean blue,
  She's a box of chewing tu-lu
For each one in Honolu'.
  I wish she'd bring some back to me and you.

1890

NOTE ON THE TEXTS
& ILLUSTRATIONS

The 81 song lyrics in this collection are arranged first by genre and then by author; Stephen Foster's songs are presented at the beginning of each generic section, and other authors' songs follow in order of the date of composition or first publication of each author's earliest included work. (The one exception is "Oh My Darling Clementine" by Percy Montrose, which follows H. S. Thompson's "Down by the River Lived a Maiden," on which it is based.)

The texts of the lyrics have mainly been taken from the earliest known editions of the sheet music; in eight instances, lyrics have been reprinted from other sources, including periodicals and book editions of the lyricists' works. Some minor emendations have been made in the course of rendering the sheet music texts as song lyrics: line breaks have been added, dashes and other marks used to indicate musical phrasing have been omitted ("ev_ _ 'ry" becomes "ev'ry"), and terminal punctuation or letter case has very occasionally been altered to fit the verse form. Otherwise, the texts are presented without change, apart from the correction of typographical errors. Unconventional spelling and punctuation, particularly in dialect and comic songs, may be expressive features, and they have not been altered.

The following is a list of the sources from which the texts have been taken:

Plantation Melodies

STEPHEN C. FOSTER

Lou'siana Belle: *Lou'siana Belle* (Cincinnati: W. C. Peters, 1847).

Uncle Ned: *Songs of the Sable Harmonists* (Louisville: W. C. Peters, 1848).

Susanna: *Songs of the Sable Harmonists* (Louisville: W. C. Peters, 1848).

Away Down Souf: *Songs of the Sable Harmonists* (Louisville: W. C. Peters, 1848).

Nelly Was a Lady: *Foster's Ethiopian Melodies* (New York: Firth, Pond & Co., 1849).

Nelly Bly: *Nelly Bly* (New York: Firth, Pond & Co., 1850)

"Gwine to Run All Night," or De Camptown Races: *Foster's Plantation Melodie* (Baltimore: F. D. Benteen, 1850).

Angelina Baker: *Foster's Plantation Melodies* (Baltimore: F. D. Benteen, 1850).

Ring, Ring de Banjo!: *Ring de Banjo: New Ethiopian Melody* (New York: Firth, Pond & Co. 1851).

Old Folks at Home: *Old Folks at Home: Ethiopian Melody* (New York: Firth, Pond & Co., 1851).

Massa's in de Cold Ground: *Massa's In De Cold Ground* (New York: Firth, Pond & Co.,1852).

My Old Kentucky Home, Good-Night: *My Old Kentucky Home, Good-Night: Foster's Plantation Melodies, No. 20* (New York: Firth, Pond & Co., 1853).

The Glendy Burk: *Foster's Plantation Melodies No. 48* (New York: Firth, Pond & Co., 1860).

Old Black Joe: *Foster's Melodies No. 49* (New York: Firth, Pond & Co., 1860).

THOMAS DARTMOUTH "DADDY" RICE

Jim Crow: *Jim Crow* (New York: E. Riley, n.d. [c. 1832]).

GEORGE WASHINGTON DIXON (ATTRIBUTION DISPUTED)

Zip Coon: *Zip Coon* (New York: J. L. Hewitt, n.d. [c. 1834]).

My Long Tail Blue: *My Long Tail Blue* (New York: J. L. Hewitt, n.d. [c. 1834]).

DANIEL DECATUR EMMETT

Old Dan Tucker: *Old Dan Tucker* (Boston: C. H. Keith, 1843).

I wish I was in Dixie's Land: *Dixie's Land* (New York: Firth, Pond & Co., 1860).

"J. K."

The Yellow Rose of Texas: *The Yellow Rose of Texas* (New York: Firth, Pond & Co., 1858).

HENRY CLAY WORK

Kingdom Coming: *Kingdom Coming* (Chicago: Root & Cady, 1862).

JAMES A. BLAND

Carry Me Back to Old Virginny: *Carry Me Back to Old Virginny* (Boston: John F. Perry & Co., 1878).

Oh, Dem Golden Slippers!: *Oh, Dem Golden Slippers!* (Boston: John F. Perry & Co., 1879).

In the Evening by the Moonlight: *In the Evening by the Moonlight* (New York: Benjamin W. Hitchcock, 1880).

Parlor Ballads

STEPHEN C. FOSTER

Ah! May the Red Rose Live Alway!: *Ah! May the Red Rose Live Alway!* (Baltimore: F. D. Benteen, 1850).

I Would Not Die in Spring Time: *I Would Not Die in Spring Time* (Baltimore: F. D. Benteen, 1850).

Old Dog Tray: *Foster's American Melodies, No. 21* (New York: Firth, Pond & Co., 1853).

Jeanie with the Light Brown Hair: *Foster's American Melodies, No. 26* (New York: Firth, Pond & Co., 1854).

Gentle Annie: *Foster's American Melodies, No. 31* (New York: Firth, Pond & Co., 1856).

Linger in Blissful Repose: *Foster's American Melodies, No. 34* (New York: Firth, Pond & Co., 1858).

Beautiful Dreamer: *Beautiful Dreamer* (New York: William A. Pond & Co., 1864).

Kiss Me Mother Ere I Die: *Kiss Me Mother Ere I Die* (New York: William A. Pond & Co., 1869).

JOHN HOWARD PAYNE

Home! Sweet Home!: *Home! Sweet Home!* (Philadelphia: G. E. Blake., [c. 1823]).

GEORGE POPE MORRIS

Woodman! Spare That Tree!: *Woodman! Spare that Tree!* (New York: Firth & Hall, 1837). Morris titled his lyrics "The Oak" when he published them in his collection *The Deserted Bride and Other Poems* (New York: Adlard & Saunders, 1838).

HENRY D. L. WEBSTER

Lorena: *Three Beautiful Ballads* (Chicago: Higgins Brothers, 1857).

W. W. FOSDICK

Aura Lee: *Aura Lee* (New York: Firth, Pond & Co., 1861).

WILL S. HAYS

I'll Remember You, Love, in My Prayers: *Poems and Songs* (Louisville: Chas. T. Dearing, 1895), pp. 107–8. Originally published in sheet music form as "I'll Remember You in My Prayers" (New York: John L. Peters, 1869).

BREWSTER HIGLEY

Western Home: *Kirwin Chief* (Kirwin, Kansas), February 26, 1876. For the publication history of this song, see Kirke Mechem, "Home on the Range," *Kansas Historical Quarterly*, November 1949. Written in 1872 or early 1873, it was probably first published in December 1873, in an issue of *The Smith County Pioneer* (Kansas) no longer extant, as "Oh, Give Me a Home Where the Buffalo Roam."

HENRY CLAY WORK

Grandfather's Clock: *Grandfather's Clock* (Boston: Oliver Ditson & Co., 1876).

Drinking and Temperance Songs

STEPHEN C. FOSTER

Willie We Have Missed You: *Foster's Melodies, No. 25* (New York: Firth, Pond & Co., 1854).

Comrades Fill No Glass for Me: *Comrades Fill No Glass for Me* (Baltimore: Miller & Beacham, 1855).

The Wife: *Foster's Melodies, No. 43* (New York: Firth, Pond & Co., 1860).

JESSE HUTCHINSON JR.

King Alcohol: *King Alcohol, a Comic Temperance Glee* (Boston: Oliver Ditson, 1843).

HENRY CLAY WORK

"Come Home, Father!": *"Come Home, Father!"* (Chicago: Root & Cady, 1864).

JOSEPH EASTBURN WINNER

The Little Brown Jug: *The Little Brown Jug* (Philadelphia: J. E. Winner, 1869).

EDWARD HARRIGAN

I'll Never Get Drunk Any More: *I'll Never Get Drunk Any More* (Boston: White, Smith & Co., 1874).

Songs of Protest and Poverty

STEPHEN C. FOSTER

Hard Times Come Again No More: *Foster's Melodies, No. 28* (New York: Firth, Pond & Co., 1854).

The Little Ballad Girl: *Clark's School Visitor* (December 1860), p. 24.

JESSE HUTCHINSON JR.

Get off the Track!: *"Get off the Track!": A Song for Emancipation* (Boston: Jesse Hutchinson Jr. 1844).

Eight Dollars a Day: *Eight Dollars a Day* (Boston: Oliver Ditson, 1848).

CHARLES P. SHIRAS

The Popular Creed: *Book of Words of the Hutchinson Family* (New York: Baker, Godwin, 1853), pp. 51–52. Shiras published his poem "The Popular Credo," in four stanzas of 10 lines each, in *The Redemption of Labor, and Other Poems* (Pittsburgh: W. H. Whitney, 1852); the Hutchinsons adapted this or perhaps another version of the text for their song "The Popular Creed."

FRANCES D. GAGE

A Hundred Years Hence: *History of Woman Suffrage*, Elizabeth Cady Stanton, Susan B. Anthony, & Matilda Joslyn Gage, eds. (Rochester: Susan B. Anthony, 1886), pp. 38–39. Written 1852.

SOLON ROBINSON

The Dying Words of Little Katy; or, Will He Come: *The Dying Words of Little Katy; or, Will He Come* (New York: Horace Waters, 1853).

BENJAMIN HANBY

Darling Nelly Gray: *Darling Nelly Gray* (Boston: Oliver Ditson, 1858).

EDWARD HARRIGAN

McNally's Row of Flats: *McNally's Row of Flats, as Sung in Ed. Harrigan's New Play "The McSorleys"* (New York: William A. Pond & Co., 1882).

No Wealth Without Labor: *Songs in Edward Harrigan's New Comedy, "The Grip"* (New York: William A. Pond & Co., 1885).

War Songs

STEPHEN C. FOSTER

That's What's the Matter: *Foster's Melodies, No. 56* (New York: Firth, Pond & Co., 1862).

Was My Brother in the Battle?: *Foster's Melodies, No. 10* (New York: Horace Waters, 1862).

SAMUEL WOODWORTH

New-Orleans (The Hunters of Kentucky): "New-Orleans," *Ladies' Literary Cabinet*, February 10, 1821. Later published in sheet music form as "The Hunters of Kentucky."

JOHN HILL HEWITT

The Minstrel's Returned from the War: John H. Hewitt, *Miscellaneous Poems* (Baltimore: N. Hickman, 1838), pp. 159–60.

HENRY S. WASHBURN

The Vacant Chair: *The Vacant Chair* (Chicago: Root & Cady, 1861).

GEORGE F. ROOT

Just Before the Battle, Mother: *Just Before the Battle, Mother* (Chicago: Root and Cady, 1862).

Tramp! Tramp! Tramp! (The Prisoner's Hope): *Tramp! Tramp! Tramp!* (Chicago: Root & Cady, 1862).

MARIE RAVENAL DE LA COSTE

Somebody's Darling: *Somebody's Darling* (Macon, Georgia: J. C. Schreiner & Son, 1864).

WALTER KITTREDGE

Tenting on the Old Camp Ground: *Tenting on the Old Camp Ground* (Boston: Oliver Ditson & Co., 1864).

HENRY CLAY WORK

Marching Through Georgia: *Our National War Songs: Marching Through Georgia* (Cleveland: S. Brainard's Sons, 1865).

EDWARD HARRIGAN

The Regular Army O!: *The Regular Army O!* (New York: William A. Pond & Co., 1874).

Comic Songs

GEORGE COOPER (LYRICS); STEPHEN C. FOSTER (MUSIC)

My Wife Is a Most Knowing Woman: *Foster's Melodies, No. 19* (New York: Horace Waters, 1863).

If You've Only Got a Moustache: *Foster's Melodies, No. 18* (New York: Horace Waters, 1864).

Mr. & Mrs. Brown: *Foster's Melodies, No. 21* (New York: Horace Waters, 1864).

WILLIAM STARK

The Modern Belle: *Book of Words of the Hutchinson Family* (New York: Baker, Godwin, 1853), pp. 53–54. The lyrics of the Hutchinsons' "Modern Belle"—credited to "General Starke"—were taken from a longer poem by William Stark (1825–1873) delivered at a centennial celebration at Manchester, New Hampshire, on October 22, 1851, and published in part in *The Farmer's Cabinet* (Amherst, New Hampshire) on October 29, 1851.

H. S. THOMPSON

Down by the River Lived a Maiden: *Down by the River Lived a Maiden* (Boston: Oliver Ditson & Co., 1863).

PERCY MONTROSE

Oh My Darling Clementine: *Oh My Darling Clementine* (Boston: Oliver Ditson & Co., 1884).

SEPTIMUS WINNER

Der Deitcher's Dog: *Der Deitcher's Dog* (Philadelphia: Sep. Winner & Co., 1864).

"BLASEE"

The Girl That Keeps the Peanut Stand: *The Girl that Keeps the Peanut Stand* (Philadelphia: W. R. Smith, 1868).

EDWARD HARRIGAN

Sweet Mary Ann: *Sweet Mary Ann* (New York: William A. Pond & Co., 1878).

Down in Gossip Row: *Down in Gossip Row* (New York: William A. Pond & Co., 1880).

Cash! Cash! Cash!: *Cash! Cash! Cash!* (New York: William A. Pond & Co., 1881).

BILLY MORTIMER

Fifty Cents: *Dan Lewis' Popular Songs of the Day* (Boston: White, Smith & Co., 1881).

JOSEPH FLYNN

Down Went McGinty: *Down Went McGinty* (New York: Spaulding & Kornder, 1889).

Globe Trotting Nellie Bly: *Globe Trotting Nellie Bly* (New York: Willis Woodward & Co., 1890).

The illustrations accompanying the present volume have been taken from a number of sources, as follows:

Frontispiece: STEPHEN C. FOSTER (c. 1859–60). Foster Hall Collection, Center for American Music, University of Pittsburgh Library System. Reprinted by permission.

Plantation Melodies: TWO MINSTREL ARCHETYPES: "JIM CROW" (c. 1832), BY THOMAS DARTMOUTH "DADDY" RICE, AND "ZIP COON" (c. 1834), ATTRIBUTED TO G. W. DIXON. Yale Collection of American Literature, Beinecke Rare Book and Manuscript Library: "Mr. T. Rice as the original Jim Crow," JWJ Sheet Music V4 R357 J5643; "Zip Coon," 2001 Folio S8 V1 Z67. Reprinted by permission.

Parlor Ballads: FOSTER'S "JEANIE WITH THE LIGHT BROWN HAIR" (1854). Lester S. Levy Collection of Sheet Music, Special Collections at the Sheridan Libraries of the Johns Hopkins University, Box 067, Item 067.086. Reprinted by permission.

Drinking and Temperance Songs: FOSTER'S "COMRADES, FILL NO GLASS FOR ME" (1855) AND JOSEPH EASTBURN WINNER'S "THE LITTLE BROWN JUG" (1869). "Comrades, Fill No Glass for Me": Lester S. Levy Collection of Sheet Music, Special Collections at the Sheridan Libraries of the Johns Hopkins University, Box 067, Item 067.26. Reprinted by permission. "The Little Brown Jug": Historic American Sheet Music B-257, Rare Book, Manuscript, and Special Collections Library, Duke University Libraries. Reprinted by permission.

Songs of Poverty and Protest: THE HUTCHINSON FAMILY SINGERS (c. 1843). Lester S. Levy Collection of Sheet Music, Special Collections at the Sheridan Libraries of the Johns Hopkins University, Box 018, Item 018.058. Reprinted by permission.

Songs of War: SAMUEL WOODWORTH'S "THE HUNTERS OF KENTUCKY" (1824). Lester S. Levy Collection of Sheet Music, Special Collections at the Sheridan Libraries of the Johns Hopkins University, Box 014, Item 014.001. Reprinted by permission.

Comic Songs: EDWARD HARRIGAN (c. 1880). Billy Rose Theatre Collection, New York Public Library, Billy Rose Theatre Collection, Image ID TH-19090. Reprinted by permission.

NOTES

In the notes below, the reference numbers denote page and line of this volume (the line count includes headings). No note is made for material included in standard desk-reference works. Biblical quotations are keyed to the King James Version. Quotations from Shakespeare are keyed to *The Riverside Shakespeare*, ed. G. Blakemore Evans (Boston: Houghton Mifflin, 1974).

4.14   Polka pigeon wing]   The polka arrived in America, from Prague via Paris, in 1844. The pigeon wing, a dance that consisted primarily of shaking one leg in the air, was associated with African Americans and minstrel performers, and contributed the "wing" to "buck and wing" dancing.

4.17   Dandy Jim ob Caroline]   "Dandy Jim from Caroline" was a popular minstrel song published in 1844 and the precursor of LaVern Baker's 1957 rhythm-and-blues hit "Jim Dandy" (written by Lincoln Chase).

6.1   Susanna]   Susanna was the middle name of Foster's beloved and musically talented older sister, Charlotte, who died in 1829 of "bilious fever" and may make a ghostly reappearance in this song's third verse.

6.10–12   the telegraph . . . bulgine bust]   The "telegraph" on which the singer jumps was a steamboat, *Telegraph No. 1* or *No. 2*, which plied the Ohio River. "Lectrick fluid" conflates the telegraph's current with steam power. A "bulgine" is a locomotive's steam engine. This racist verse dramatizes how these three technological advances—the steamboat, the locomotive, and the telegraph—annihilated not only African Americans but all time and space.

7.9   juba]   An African-American dance imitated and popularized by minstrel performers, including a black dancer, William Henry Lane, who took "Juba" as his stage name and astounded Charles Dickens when the novelist visited New York.

9.15   dulcem]   Sweet.

10.14   Camptown]   Although a Camptown exists in Pennsylvania, and Irvington, New Jersey, originally bore this name, "Camptown" was also a generic term for an outlying, makeshift settlement, the kind of out-of-bounds place where horse races, illegal in many jurisdictions, were often held.

10.26   bob-tail nag]   A horse with a cropped tail, like the "bobtail" in James Pierpont's "The One Horse Open Sleigh," or "Jingle Bells," published seven years later.

12.13   jawbone]   A primitive percussion instrument usually fashioned from the jaw of a horse, mule, or donkey.

12.26   wellumscope]   A comic garbling of "telescope."

15.12   Swanee ribber]   Foster originally wrote "*Pedee* ribber," but a popular minstrel song already invoked this river in South Carolina, so he eventually substituted northern Florida's (and southern Georgia's) Suwannee. Foster never set eyes on either river.

18.1   My Old Kentucky Home, Good-Night!]   Inspired by Harriet Beecher Stowe's antislavery novel *Uncle Tom's Cabin*, Foster titled the first draft of this song "Poor Uncle Tom, Good Night."

19.4   totter on the road]   An echo of Robert Burns's "John Anderson My Jo": "Now we maun totter down, John, / And hand in hand we'll go, / And sleep the gither at the foot, / John Anderson my Jo."

19.7   The Glendy Burk]   Far from being a "mighty fast boat," the *Glendy Burke* hit a snag and broke up near Cairo, Illinois, five years before Foster wrote this song.

21.18   Tuckyhoe]   An area in tidewater Virginia, though it is frequently identified with Kentucky.

22.5   Pagannini]   Niccolò Paganini (1782–1840), the Italian virtuoso violinist.

22.10   Packenham]   Major-General Sir Edward Michael Pakenham (1778–1815), commander of the British army in North America during the War of 1812, was defeated and died in the Battle of New Orleans.

22.19   Calaboose]   Jail, from the Louisiana French *calabouse* and the Spanish *calabozo*.

23.2   I wip my weight in wildcats] A frontier boast associated with Davy Crockett.

23.5   Dan kiver]   Than cover.

24.25   Massa Hays] Jacob Hayes, a protégé of Aaron Burr, was high constable of New York City from 1802 to 1850.

26.22   Hoboken]   Directly across the Hudson River from Manhattan, Hoboken, New Jersey, was home to the Elysian Fields, a pleasure garden where minstrels and other entertainers frequently performed.

27.12   Weehawk]   Weehawken, New Jersey, borders Hoboken.

27.17–23   de museum . . . hunkie] John Scudder's New American Museum, later purchased by P. T. Barnum, included among its exhibits wax figures of "the Sleeping Beauty, with her infant" and "David Lambert, the Mammoth Man." Lambert (1770–1809) was a famously fat Englishman who weighed 739 pounds. The meaning of "a skeleton on he hunkie" is obscure, though it may refer to Calvin Edson (c. 1788–c. 1833), a "living skeleton" or "walking skeleton" who was exhibited at the museum around 1830. "Hunk" or "hunker," in the early 19th century, could mean "wretch" or "miser," a sense that might fit such a reference.

28.12   De great Nullification] John C. Calhoun and South Carolina asserted states' rights in 1832 by nullifying a federal tariff and threatening to secede if the national government attempted to collect customs duties by force.

30.18   Zip Coon]   George Washington Dixon probably did not originate this song or the role for which he became well-known. "Zip Coon" may have been composed by George Nichols or Robert Farrell, who were blackface circus clowns, or a "Mr. Palmer," who was advertised as performing it. The melody remains familiar to this day as the tune of "Turkey in the Straw."

The song was published in a number of different versions. Another (New York: Thomas Birch, 1834) varies in verses 4–6:

4

I tell you what will happen den, now bery soon,
De Nited States Bank will be blone to de moon;
Dare General Jackson, will him lampoon,
An de bery nex President, will be Zip Coon.

5

An wen Zip Coon our President shall be,
He make all de little Coons sing posum up a Tree;
O how de little Coons, will dance and sing,
Wen he tie dare tails togedder, cross de lim dey swing.

Now mind wat you arter, you tarnel kritter Crocket,
You shant go head widout old Zip, he is de boy to block it,
Zip shall be President, Crocket shall be vice,
And den dey two togedder, will hab de tings nice.

30.22   posum up a gum tree]   "Possum up a Gum Tree, Coony in the Holler" was a popular song among African Americans. An English visitor to New York City in the early 1820s reported hearing it sung in a black theater, where it interrupted a soliloquy in *Hamlet*.

31.4   O Zip a duden]   An antecedent of the "Doo-dah!" sung by Foster's Camptown ladies; of "Zip-a-Dee-Doo-Dah," written by Allie Wrubel and Ray Gilbert and sung by Johnny Mercer in Walt Disney's animated *The Song of the South*; and of the Crystals' "Da Doo Ron Ron," written by Ellie Greenwich, Jeff Barry, and Phil Spector.

32.5   Old Packenham]   See note 22.10.

32.13   My Long Tail Blue]   Again, Dixon popularized this song but may not have composed it. The garment in question is a swallow-tailed coat, the height of fashionable menswear in the 1830s and '40s.

34.8   Old Dan Tucker]   A version of this song published in *The Celebrated Negro Melodies, as Sung by the Virginia Minstrels* (Boston: George P. Reed, 1843) varies substantially:

I come to town de oder night,
I look'd around I seed a sight
De Watchmen dey assembled round
Oh! Hark! Ole Tucker is come to town.

CHORUS
Get out de way, get out de way, get out de way
Now Ole Dan Tucker you're too late to come to supper.

2
Here's my razor in good order
Magnum bonum just a border
Sheep shell de oats ole Tucker shell de corn
And I shave you soon as my water warm.

3
De niggers dey come far and near
To hear him play dis ole banjo
He used to sit by de light ob de moon
And fire away dis good ole tune.

4

Ole Tucker lib in a little log hut
His face it was de color ob sut
His nose was flat his eye was full
And his head looked like a bag of wool.

5

Ole Tucker didn't come from Guinea
But he libed in ole Virginny
He used to lib on so much fat
Dat his head so big he couldn't wear a hat.

6

I went up to Keeple steeple
Dare I met some colored people
Some was brack and some was bracker
Some was de color ob brown tobacco.

7

Way down in ole Beaver creek
De niggers grow some ten or leven feet
Dey go to bed but it aint no use
For dare feet hang out for de chicken foost.

8

Sheep and hog walking in de paster
Knife and fork a sticking in dare shoulder
Wonder where is ole Dan Tucker
To come and kill dis hog for supper.

9

Dare was a nigger in our town
He swallowed a hogshead molasses down
De molasses worked de hogshead bust
And he went up in a thunder gust.

34.18   darby ram]   "The Derby Ram" is a traditional English comic
    folk song.
35.3   Magnum bonum]   A variety of apple originating in North Car-
    olina was dubbed a "magnum bonum," as were an English plum and,
    later, a potato, but here it probably means that the singer's razor is a
    "great good," the best money can buy.

36.1   Dixie's Land]   The origins of the word "Dixie" are disputed. It seems not to have been widely used to designate the South before this song became popular on both sides of the Mason-Dixon Line ("Dixon" being one of several possible sources of the moniker). In *Way Up North in Dixie: A Black Family's Claim to the Confederate Anthem* (Washington, D.C.: Smithsonian Institution Press, 1993), Howard L. Sacks and Judith Rose Sacks discuss local traditions attributing the authorship of "Dixie" to the Snowden family of Mount Vernon, Ohio.

36.19   'forty-pound'er]   A cannon (or cannonball) commonly used in naval and coastal warfare.

39.8   Linkum gumboats]   Yankee (Abraham Lincoln's) gunboats.

39.15   Jubilo]   Jubilee, in Hebrew scripture (Leviticus 25:10–55, and elsewhere) a celebration held every 50 years during which debts are forgiven and slaves are freed.

39.24   contraband]   Slaves who escaped or were captured by Union forces were recognized as "contraband of war" and not returned to their Southern owners.

41.24   chariot in de morn]   The chariot of fire that bore the prophet Elijah to heaven (2 Kings, 2:11–12) and inspired the African-American spiritual "Swing Low, Sweet Chariot."

42.10   de golden street]   In the Book of Revelation (21:21), the street of Heaven, or New Jerusalem, "was pure gold."

42.23   ulster coats]   Heavy overcoats of coarse fabric that ward off the wind and cold.

50.15   I Would Not Die in Spring Time]   Foster followed up this song, issued under the pseudonym of Milton Moore, with "I Would Not Die in Summer Time," for which he used his own name. John Hill Hewitt published a parody, "I Would Not Die at All."

56.13   lorelie]   A legendary German siren whose song lured sailors to their deaths; celebrated in a poem by Heinrich Heine that Franz Liszt and Friedrich Silcher set to music.

66.7   Solomon vale]   Solomon is a small town in Kansas. These lyrics first appeared in a newspaper in Kansas, which eventually adopted "Home on the Range" as its state song.

66.9   the Beaver]   Beaver Creek is in southwestern Kansas.

76.13   Tom and Jerry]   A potent punch, usually concocted with rum.

76.13   Perry]   Fermented pear juice.

82.22   budge]   Slang for strong drink.

82.24   to take Giberalter]   Britain's imperial outpost of Gibraltar was impregnable.

89.17   *Clay* foundation]   A slap at the efforts of Kentucky senator Henry Clay, "the Great Compromiser," to preserve the Union by accommodating slavery.

89.18   *"The Magician"*]   Democratic President Martin Van Buren.

96.15   Millenium]   In Revelation 20, an angel casts Satan into a bottomless pit so that "he should deceive the nations no more, till the thousand years should be fulfilled." Various 19th-century religious and secular groups believed this millennium of peace and harmony was drawing near.

97.4   hot corn]   Not popcorn but a roasted ear of corn, frequently sold by street vendors.

101.3   McNally's Row of Flats]   This song was originally written for the play *The McSorleys*.

101.6   gossoons]   Boys, an Irish adaption of the French *garçons*.

101.20   Lazaronees]   Rascals, rabble, from the Italian *lazzarone*.

102.7   No Wealth Without Labor]   This song was originally written for the play *The Grip*.

109.11–15   Merrimac . . . Ericsson]   The Confederacy's *Merrimac* (also spelled *Merrimack* and known as CSS *Virginia*) and the North's *Monitor*, which was designed and built by John Ericsson, were ironclad warships that clashed off Hampton Roads, Virginia, in March 1862.

109.20   Gen'ral Beauregard]   General P.G.T. Beauregard (1818–1893) led the Confederates to victory in the First Battle of Bull Run.

110.17–18   the noble Highland host]   The 79th New York Volunteer Infantry, a Scottish-American regiment called the Highlanders, took part in the invasion of South Carolina in early 1862 and incurred heavy casualties in a failed attempt to capture Charleston.

111.2   when the flag of Erin came]   The Irish Brigade, originally comprising three New York infantry regiments of predominantly Irish-American volunteers, fought valiantly in the Peninsula Campaign during the spring and summer of 1862.

111.13   New-Orleans (The Hunters of Kentucky)]   When it was first published, in the *Ladies' Literary Cabinet* on February 10, 1821, Woodworth's song was titled "New-Orleans." It was prefaced with a brief note to the publisher: "The following song was written at the request of our late friend *Hopkins Robertson*, who intended to have sung it, in the character and dress of a Kentucky Rifleman, at his last benefit, but was prevented by death. If you think it worth publishing, it is at your service." The song (to be sung to the tune "Miss Bailey") was later retitled "The Hunters of Kentucky."

112.10   Packenham]   See note 22.10.

118.6   the "Battle-Cry of Freedom,"]   A plug for an extremely popular song Root had composed at the outset of the Civil War.

124.12   forninst]   Gaelic: in front of, against.

125.20   Chafe]   Chief.

126.20   Zoo-zoos]   The French Zouaves, infantry that served primarily in North Africa and sported open-fronted jackets, baggy pants, flamboyant sashes, and exotic headgear, were emulated by various American regiments during and after the Civil War.

147.10   old Hoyle]   Edmond Hoyle (1672–1769), an authority on the rules of games.

147.18   alamande]   Allemande, a popular dance in triple meter.

148.1   Down in Gossip Row]   This song was originally written for the play *The Mulligan Guard Nominee*.

150.1   Cash! Cash! Cash!]   This song was originally written for the play *Mordecai Lyons*.

155.4   John the Great]   Probably the Irish-American boxing champion John L. Sullivan.

157.2   Nellie Bly]   Elizabeth Jane Cochran (1864–1922) was a pioneering female journalist. Born outside Pittsburgh the year Foster died, she borrowed her byline from Foster's "Nelly Bly."

157.18   "La Grippe"]   Influenza.

157.25   Gaiety dance]   Named after the New York City theater where it allegedly originated, this vaudeville dance entailed swirling a long, flouncy skirt to reveal enticing glimpses of leg.

INDEX OF LYRICISTS, COMPOSERS, TITLES, AND FIRST LINES

AMERICAN POETS PROJECT